Praise for *In Changing Times*

Ron Higdon has drawn on his fifty years of ministry experience to suggest ways interim ministers can deal with the illusions, anxieties, conflicts and communication problems in the churches where they serve. Higdon offers a clear and honest appraisal of how to understand the dynamics of congregations and how one can provide helpful leadership during the interim time. This book provides a needed resource tool for interim ministers. I commend it highly.

William Powell Tuck, Interim Pastor
Westover Baptist Church, Richmond, VA

Upon hearing him preach regularly, a seminary professor of theology commented that Ron Higdon could take a complicated theological concept and put it in a sentence that could be easily digested. In this writing Ron brings this gift to the table set with transition times in the life of congregations. He is clear, to the point, biblically sound and realistic. He prepares the menu from the perspective of vast ministry background and what he has experienced as best for a congregation seeking health and wholeness for its divinely-given journey.

Bob Ivan Johnson, Ph.D
Interim ministry specialist and church consultant

Being "too soon old and too late smart," Ron Higdon offers valuable insights for ministry, Christian leadership, and growing as a disciple of Christ. He invites readers to become conversation partners in a journey of thought and self-reflection. He writes as a pastor, a scholar, a leader, and a lifelong learner. His insights are exciting and affirming; we are all pilgrims journeying together. He is a modern-day prophet, savvy enough to know that the future is not as important as today yet that the future depends on what we do today.

Bo Prosser, Ed.D.
Coordinator of Organizational Relationships
Cooperative Baptist Fellowship

Ron Higdon is right: "the time to discuss the characteristics of a healthy church is … NOW!" Drawing upon decades of experience and his discipline to be reflective and thoughtfully observant, Higdon has created an entertaining and insightful guide to life in the real world of congregations. Blending biblical and conventional wisdom with relevant stories and experiences has produced a superb guide toward a healthy ministry and church. Thank you, Ron, for this diary/map/motivational message!

Bill Wilson
Director, The Center for Healthy Churches

The title of this book is a good clue to its valuable content—especially when you realize Ron Higdon has seen "changing times" in life and ministry for more than a half century. Unlike some who quit reading and learning once they receive their diploma, Ron Hidgon has been a life long learner. *In Changing Times: A Guide for Reflection and Conversation* reveals that the author is a voracious reader of books **and** people and situations.

The sub-title of his book is also telling; it provides a good clue that the author respects the views of others and invites conversation. The author provides a role-model for congregations in this regard. What better way for congregations to face their ever-changing and challenging landscape than to apply the words of the last chapter: "Major on Conversation, Candor, and Compassion."

The author achieves his goal by providing tools for pastors and church leaders as they deal with "anxiety and conflict and an understanding of church dynamics." This is a book "tool" you will read and re-read, mark and re-mark, dogear and reach for repeatedly to recover that much needed insight and quote.

John Lepper
Retired Coordinator, Kentucky Baptist Fellowship

In Changing Times

A Guide for Reflection and Conversation

Ronald Higdon

Guides to Practical Ministry, Volume 2
Robert D. Cornwall, General Editor

Energion Publications
Gonzalez, FL
2015

Copyright © 2015, Ronald Higdon

Unless otherwise notated, Scripture quotations are from New Revised Standard Version Bible, copyright © 1989 National Council of the Churches of Christ in the United States of America. Used by permission. All rights reserved.

Scripture quotations marked NLT are taken from the Holy Bible, New Living Translation, copyright © 1996, 2004, 2007, 2013 by Tyndale House Foundation. Used by permission of Tyndale House Publishers, Inc., Carol Stream, Illinois 60188. All rights reserved.

Cover Design: Jody Neufeld
Cover Image Credits:
   © Sepavo | Dreamstime.com - Stained Glass Photo
   (1557015)
   © Lorna | Dreamstime.com - Fists
   (818348)

ISBN10: 1-63199-153-0
ISBN13: 978-1-63199-153-0
Library of Congress Control Number: 2015938149

Energion Publications
P. O. Box 841
Gonzalez, FL 32560
850-525-3916

energion.com
pubs@energion.com

Table of Contents

Series Preface vii
Preface...ix
Introduction 1
1 Truth Is only the Beginning of the Journey 15
2 The Big Picture Provides Perspective 27
3 Control Is in Short Supply... 37
4 Beliefs and Attitudes Shape Our World 49
5 Forget about Perfection 61
6 The Dangers in Listening for the Applause 73
7 Life Is Full of Endings 83
8 We Need Eyes that See and Ears that Hear 95
9 Reflection Is Not an Option 105
10 Major on Conversation, Candor, and Compassion 115
   Insights from the Book of Proverbs 127
   Bibliography of Quoted Sources 135

Acknowledgments

This book includes a number of incidents drawn from churches I served; I have attempted to disguise the situations but some will quickly recognize their congregation. This is another one of those times in which I find it easier to ask for forgiveness than for permission! I have attempted to be "pastoral" in my assessments and as non-judgmental as possible. My purpose is to use concrete illustrations that provide the necessary "earthiness" for the truths I am attempting to share. My wife would call this "taking it out of the box."

I dedicated my book, *In the Meantime*, to all the congregations with whom I have worked. My gratitude to all of them for their support, encouragement, and opportunities for "learning on the job" only increases with the years. Nothing written here is intended to be dismissive; I still believe every place I served was a part of God's providence for my life and ministry. It was where I was meant to be at the time; my regret is that I could not bring the wisdom of later times to every aspect of my ministry then. Unlike those who have perfect 20/20 hindsight, mine is probably still more like 20/40. My plea for mercy is that I did the best I could for where I was, with what I had. Even now, although I believe I see much more clearly, like Paul, I continue to see *in a mirror dimly* (1 Corinthians 13:12).

Although many of these ideas were whirling about in my head, I had been unable to find the best organizing principle. In a dinner conversation, Jim Lemon asked why I didn't write a book in plain language based on my experiences that would help congregations deal with the problems and conflicts that are so much a part of any community's life together. I knew immediately that is what I needed to do. Much of what I learned through intentional interim and consultant training was not a part of my basic seminary education. There seemed to be too few publications that brought the tools for dealing with anxiety and conflict, and an understanding of church dynamics, into the market place of everyday church experience for both pastor and congregant. This is what this book seeks to do. In plain language you will read about what I wish I had known from the beginning of my ministry but what you can and should know right now regardless of your church size or situation. A basic truth is that people are people.

Throughout this book I suggest some "possible" activities. Almost all of these are things I have done with congregations during intentional interims. They are listed as "possible" because each church is unique; selection and adaptation are required; one size never fits all. You will, no doubt, be able to come up with improved and different activities from the ones listed. I would appreciate hearing about them. (Contact information appears at the end of the book.)

Each section concludes with five "Questions for Reflection and Discussion."

Series Preface

Clergy, having left Seminary, quickly discover that there is much about congregational ministry that they never learned in school. They have touched upon it in a practical ministry class or a preaching class, and an internship may have allowed a person to get their feet wet, but as important as this foundational education is, there is much that must be learned on the job. It is not until one spends actual time in congregational ministry that one's strengths and weaknesses are revealed. Continuing education is therefore a must. Having collegial relationships is also a must. Who else but other clergy truly understand the demands of this vocation? In addition to ongoing continuing education and collegial relationships, it is helpful to have access to books and articles authored by experienced clergy.

This series of books, the second to be sponsored by the Academy of Parish Clergy, is designed to provide clergy with resources written by practitioners – that is by people who have significant experience with ministry in local congregations. The authors of these books may have spent time teaching at seminaries or as denominational officials, but they also know what it means to serve congregations.

The Academy of Parish Clergy, the sponsor of this book series, was founded in the late 1960s. It emerged at a time when clergy began to see themselves as professionals – on par with physicians and attorneys. As such, they not only welcomed the status that comes with professional identity, but they also embraced the concept of professional standards and training. Not only were clergy to obtain graduate degrees, but they were engage in ongoing continuing education. Following the lead of other professions, the founders of the Academy of Parish Clergy saw this new organization as being the equivalent to the American Medical Association or the American Bar Association. By becoming a member of this organization one would have access to a set of standards, a means of accountability outside denominational auspices, and have access to continuing education opportunities. These ideals remain in place to this day. The Academy stands as a beacon to clergy looking for support and accountability in an age when even the religious vocation is no longer held in high esteem.

In 2012, the Academy launched its first book series in partnership with Energion Publications. This series, entitled *Conversations in Ministry*, fits closely with an important part of the mission of the Academy – encouraging clergy to gather in groups to support one another and hold each other accountable in their local ministry settings. The books in this first series are brief (under 100 pages), making them useful for igniting conversation.

This second series, *Guides to Practical Ministry*, features longer books. Like the first series these books are written by clergy for clergy. They can be used by groups, but because they are lengthier in scope, they can go into greater depth than the books found in the first series. Books in this series will cover issues like writing sermons, interim ministry, self-care, clergy ethics, administrative tasks, the use of social media, worship leadership.

On behalf of the Academy of Parish Clergy, the series' editorial team, and the publisher, I pray that the books in this series will be a blessing to all who read them and to all who receive the ministry of these readers.

Robert D. Cornwall, APC
General Editor

Preface

"Too soon old, too late smart" (based on the Pennsylvania Dutch saying: "Ve grow too soon olt and too late schmart")[1] was foreign to my understanding in the early years. When we are young there is a strong temptation to think we have forever to accomplish our goals, or at least a very long time. A popular song when I was growing up was "It's Later than You Think." My twist on that would be: "The future got here much sooner than I expected." It always does. It hardly seems possible that I am in the second half of my seventieth decade. It is a shock to discover where old people come from – they come from us! But it's not all bad news.

"Too late smart" is too harsh a judgment. There are some things we come to understand, view differently, and simply accept only when we have had sufficient life experiences that enable us to gain a better/different perspective on things. I do believe that I have lived into some "smarts" that were not possible for me in the early years. The wise counsel of teachers and mentors I now understand with greater clarity; many things that we often complain they didn't teach us in college or seminary we now know they did – we simply didn't have the context of experience in which to see and hear them. That is also why the re-reading of books, especially the Scriptures, is so valuable. We are able to find things we never knew were there because we have lived into a different life-context. We don't berate ourselves for what we didn't see earlier; we simply weren't ready. I have found the familiar quote to be true: "When the pupil is ready, the teacher will come." I have also found Esalen's Law to be true: "You always teach others what you most need to learn yourself."[2]

One of the major "smarts" I have lived into is the realization of just how vast is the ocean of truth and how very limited is my

---

1 Tad Tuleja, *Quirky Quotations* (New York: Galahad Books, 1992), 172.
2 Rick Fields, *Chop Wood Carry Water* (Los Angeles: Jeremy P. Tarcher, 1984), 21.

knowledge and understanding. In the land of smarts, I acknowledge I'm still in the undergraduate program. Paul confesses, *"We know in part"* (I Corinthians 13:9) and perhaps it takes some living to realize this is our ongoing confession. But there were some things he did know and I do believe I have lived into some truths that seem to me basic for all of us in this journey called life. It is a little bit of wisdom I have acquired the hard way (my usual learning stance) and I even have the bruises and scars to prove it. My life has been lived in pastorates which have been my training ground. I could have titled this book "Church Truths" even though they are applicable to all of life – both personally and in community relationships.

One of my critics charged that my books are written in a conversational manner, more for the ear than for the eye. That is correct. When I am writing, I think of someone seated across from me as I attempt to talk about the things in life with which we all struggle. One of my high school English teachers once commented on a book she was reading that made her "spit cotton." A seminary preaching professor told us it was all right to impress classmates with our oratorical skills, knowledge of Hebrew and Greek, and deep theological insights (all of which were actually in short supply), but that when we stepped into the pulpit on Sunday morning our duty was to convey in clear and easily understood language the message of the text. Many of the things discussed in this book are to be found in weightier texts; my goal is to introduce a wide variety of survival (and thriving!) skills for churches that most will never encounter in general reading.

I invite you into conversation with me as I talk about some of the things I have learned in over fifty years of pastoral ministry. As I continue my work as an intentional interim minister and church consultant, I am amazed at how many congregations function on the basis of comforting illusions. Since the lessons I have learned are equally applicable to individuals, families, and all other relationships, the applications often seem quite threatening and the level of resistance quite high. In workshops, I frequently begin with a warning that I am going to write on the board a word that will shake all of them to the very foundation of their lives; if any are faint of heart they might want to exit immediately. Then I write one word on the board: "Change!" That is the most threatening and challenging word in our language. It is the most feared because we usually see it as what happens beyond control in our lives and in our world; change is seldom viewed as something we intentionally decide to do in specific ways in order to have better lives, better relationships, and better churches.

I have tried to acknowledge the sources for the many truths that fill this book but I have avoided technical terms and complicated explanations. A person once critiqued my sermon to a member of my congregation with, "Your pastor is a scholar." I don't think he intended it to be a compliment and I don't think he was correct. I consider myself to be forever learning and (hopefully) forever growing. A concept in vogue when I was a seminary student was to view the pastor as "the theologian in residence." I understand this to mean: "The work of the pastor is to help people understand the life-giving logic of the gospel of Jesus Christ in the totality of their lives."[1] If that what it means to be a scholar, so be it.

As always, I invite you to disagree, to make your comments in the margins of the book, and even send me an email (which I will answer) if you have a particular axe to grind. Allow me to rephrase the saying that begins this preface: "Older at just the right time and the place to begin to understand some of the undergirding truths of existence that I feel confident enough to share with you, not in the spirit of judgment or superiority, but with the keen awareness that we are all in this thing together and are meant to help each other in whatever ways we can." Of course, I continue to work on incorporating the wisdom truths into my daily living and in my working with congregations.

You will notice that I have listed the Scripture references under the heading of "The Biblical Witness." I could have titled the

---

[1] Ronald E. Vallet, *Stewards of the Gospel* (Grand Rapids: William B. Eerdmans, 2011), 3.

sections "Biblical Wisdom." I much prefer this to the talk about biblical principles, the Bible as rules for life or our answer book. Rules and answers sound too much like quick-fixes and easy solutions. If the Bible is basically one of principles, rules, and answers it amazes me how diverse are the principles, rules, and answers that sincere seekers find there. The real problem is once these are "discovered," it is simply a matter of imposing them on everyone else.

"The Bible says it, I believe it, that settles it" often works itself out in dogmatism, isolationism, judgmentalism, and, at its worst, terrorism. Defenders of the Bible always view themselves as defenders of the truth and, ultimately, as defenders of God. They almost never see themselves as defenders of their particular *interpretations* of Scripture.

The history of biblical interpretation brings the realization that the same texts have been seen in different ways. We continue to overlook how the prevailing culture affects biblical interpretation. Our own Civil War found sincere ministers preaching texts that plainly defended slavery. Few today would use those texts in defense of the owning and subjugating of any race. Harriet Beecher Stowe's *Uncle Tom's Cabin* questioned the prevalent idea about the self-interpreting power of the Bible.[1]

Galileo, often called the "father of modern physics," did not enjoy such acclaim during his lifetime. A literal reading of the Bible tells us that the sun moves, not the earth (Psalm 93:1; 96:10; 104:5; 1 Chronicles 16:30b; Ecclesiastes 1:4-5). The earth is seen in all places as the center of the "universe." To suggest the movement of the earth around the sun was biblical heresy. In 1632, Galileo published (with papal permission) *Dialogue Concerning the Two Chief World Systems*, but was ordered to stand trial for heresy in 1633. He was convicted and spent the remainder of his life under house arrest. It was 359 years before injustice was acknowledged. "In 1758, the general prohibition against heliocentrism was removed.

---

1   Ibid, 58.

On October 31, 1992, Pope John Paul II expressed regret for how the Galileo affair had been handled."[1]

Our revised interpretations acknowledge both the cultural context of earlier interpretations as well as the cultural context of the biblical writings. The creation account in Genesis is unique among such early accounts. In contrast to warring self-centered gods who create for their benefit, Genesis proclaims the covenant making God of Abraham, Isaac, and Jacob to be the author of all that is. And it is pronounced good. There is no concern about the how of creation; the focus is on the Who of creation. In regards to slavery, the New Testament world is not about the importation and dehumanization of one particular race. Slavery cut across all races and was the result of many circumstances. Some estimates put the number of slaves in ancient Rome at seventy percent. Many of these slaves were highly educated with varying levels of responsibility. The New Testament writers did not want the new Way in Jesus Christ to be viewed as a revolutionary movement. The biblical admonitions are calls to live exemplary, redemptive lives in order to further the witness of the gospel. Nowhere does any passage address the kind of slavery that reared its ugly head in early American history.

> How did we come to change our minds about what the texts (about slavery) actually said? What caused our churches to change course? Somehow, I think it has something to do with affirming the primacy of Jesus Christ as God's Word over and against any word or selection of words as "the Word."[2]

The one who said, "*You will know the truth and the truth will make you free,*" also said, "*I am the truth.*" What does it mean that truth is a person? What does it mean when we are told that the Word became flesh and dwelt among us? That the Word is first all of a person before it is a book? That we are called to acknowledge the living Word that comes before the written Word? My principle for biblical interpretation is that we interpret all Scripture by the

---

1   Ibid, 77.
2   Ibid, 63.

highest revelation we have, Jesus Christ. This is what the book of Hebrews is all about. The highest and clearest revelation of who God is and what he expects from us is most clearly revealed in his Son. It doesn't solve all the problems of many perplexing passages of Scripture but it lets us know where to begin.

Introduction

WHY DO WE CONTINUE TO SPEND SO MUCH TIME REARRANGING THE DECK CHAIRS?

The Biblical Witness:

> Then the Lord said to Moses, "Why do you cry out to me? Tell the Israelites to go forward." (Exodus 14:15).

> This day I call the heavens and the earth as witnesses against you that I have set before you life and death, blessings and curses. Now choose life, so that you and your children may live…. (Deuteronomy 30:19, NLT)

CONTEMPORARY OBSERVATIONS:

> Repair in the road is no longer helpful if we are headed in the wrong direction.[1]

> Resistance to change is a consistent reality in congregations.[2]

> Tacoma, age 9, in a letter to her Pastor: "I think more people would come to church if you moved it to Disneyland."[3]

LIVING ON THE BASIS OF WHAT IS

The title for this introduction comes from a popular adage (some have called it a parable) based on the sinking of the Titanic on April 15, 1912, after striking an iceberg at 11:40 p.m. the night

---

1 Jim Wallis, *Call To Conversion* (San Francisco: HarperOne, 2005), xiv.
2 Richard Blackburn, *Leadership and Anxiety in the Church* (Lombard: IL: Lombard Peace Center, 2007). From a 2011 workshop in Louisville, KY.
3 Bill Adler, *Dear Pastor* (Nashville: Thomas Nelson, 1980).

before. Walter Lord's *A Night to Remember* (1955) remains the definitive work that would have been almost unbelievable if he had written it as a piece of fiction. One hundred years later, historians continue to probe the remaining mysteries of this disaster with its loss of over 1,500 lives. The discovery of the ship's remains has changed some of the diagnoses but a few things remain the same.

For almost everyone on board that night, it was unthinkable that the Titanic could sink. The general consensus was that it was unsinkable. That is one of the major reasons there were not enough lifeboats for the 2,207 people on board. The first messages the crew and passengers received after the incident were reassuring.

> "Why have we stopped?" Lawrence Beesley asked a passing steward. "I don't know, sir," he was told, "but I don't suppose it's much." Mrs. Arthur Ryerson, of the steel family, had somewhat better results. "There's talk of an iceberg, ma'am," explained Steward Bishop, "and they have stopped, not to run over it."[1]

Most believed that in a few hours the voyage would resume. At least one passenger quipped, "Looks like we've lost a propeller, but it'll give us more time for bridge."[2] The truth is frightening: the Titanic struck the iceberg at 11:40 p.m. on Sunday night; Monday morning at 2:20 a.m. she foundered. The passengers had only two hours and twenty minutes to abandon ship. It was the only thing to be done; once the truth got out, nobody would have suggested deck chair arrangement.

An inadequate number of lifeboats, partially filled boats, no lifeboat drill, inadequate wireless communication, excessive speed, the question of binoculars, theories of human arrogance, etc. were all secondary considerations once it was learned that the ship was going to sink.

> The great question of life is: Can we choose life instead of death and then bring our choice to an effective conclusion?

---

1 Walter Lord, *A Night to Remember* (New York: St. Martin's Griffin, 2005), 10.
2 Ibid, 12.

In Changing Times

Here methods, techniques, ideas and spiritualities of themselves are of little use. We must not stand in the burning house with a dictionary thinking we are safe because we are frantically looking up the definition of a fire extinguisher.[1]

After 11:40 p.m. it didn't matter what had led to the unthinkable. It had happened and it was the single reality that had to shape everything from that moment on. The only question was: in the light of this single truth what will be our response? It was no longer possible to live on the assumption of what could never happen; it was now time to live on the basis of what had happened. Churches often find themselves in deep denial about the reality of their situation and the degree of anxiety and conflict present in the congregation. They resemble the frequently quoted, "All hope is gone. Let us pray!" When the church cries "Help!" to some outside resource, it is usually when things have reached crisis proportions. The time to seek help is when the news comes that there are icebergs in the water. When conflict reaches its highest level, it often means that the church has struck the iceberg.

ILLUSIONS ARE COMFORTING BUT NOT REALISTIC

Any person on the Titanic that fateful night eventually knew one important fact: the one necessary thing was to get off the ship as quickly as possible. Nothing else mattered. Making certain your attire was color coordinated, being certain you hadn't left any valuables in your stateroom, making certain you were in the lifeboat with people "of the right kind," getting an outside seat with a better view of the ship going down – none of these were up for consideration once the obvious issue was literally a matter of life and death.

If an auto mechanic told us, "We can't repair your brakes right now, so we just made the horn louder," would we reply, "That's fine. I'll come back next month for the brake repair"? As a piece of humor it might bring a smile, but such a suggestion is no laughing matter in the real world of motoring. It is living in the "real" world that is so problematic; we too often find ourselves residing in

---

[1] James Finley, *Merton's Palace of Nowhere* (Notre Dame: Ave Maria Press, 1978), 88.

one that is highly illusionary. Words from our friends: "Get real!" "Hello!" "Did you just get off the boat?" "What are you thinking?" "Who gave you that advice?" "Have you checked that out with anyone?" "What makes you think that will work?" are wake-up calls.

When Stephen asks, *"Which of the prophets did your ancestors not persecute?"* (Acts 7:52), he was asking a question for every generation. Contrary to popular belief, biblical prophets did not major on predicting the future. The primary role of the prophet was to announce the purpose and will of God for the present moment in history. The message was simple: "This is what God is doing in our midst right now and this is what you ought to be doing." The message was both revelation and judgment. It was usually unpopular because it called for repentance – a change of direction, a change of mind, a change of attitude – on the part of the people. Prophets made people uncomfortable.

When King Ahab greeted the prophet Elijah with the words, "Is it you, you troubler of Israel?" (I Kings 18:17), in a sense, he was right on target. That was the prophet's role – to challenge and confront those in power. The prophet stood over against the monarchy as God's corrective. Even those who don't know much of the story are aware that the name of Ahab's wife, Jezebel, represents everything you don't want to see in a ruler (or in another human being). Prophets shattered the illusions by which rulers and people lived. They often used shocking and provocative words to get the attention of those living in a dream world. When Amos addressed the wealthy women of Samaria as "You cows of Bashan who are on Mount Samaria, who oppress the poor and crush the needy, who say to their husbands, 'Bring me something to drink!'" (Amos 4:1), the response was not, "Let's invite this man to be our next Women's Club speaker." Amos was ordered out of town.

The preceding examples appear extreme because we can't imagine ourselves being like "those" people. I often say that the only time Bible study is truly effective is when we can picture ourselves in the stories, not as the heroes, but as the "villains." Our situations and our actions may not be quite as flagrant, but the prophets' message for our time is the challenge to make as honest an appraisal of our situation as we can and ask if we are responding in healthy and redemptive ways. Or, to return to the analogy, are we content to simply keep rearranging the deck chairs? Are we insistent on doing only those things that are within our comfort zones? Do we believe that things will get better without our having to do anything? Does time really heal all wounds or is it what we do in and with that time that facilitates healing? If we keep doing church business as usual will anything be different?

The time to discuss the characteristics of a healthy church, the ways and means of good communication, the best methods for dealing with conflict (in its beginning stages), et cetera, is before impending catastrophe. After a lengthy pastorate, some churches will say, "Things have gone well for thirty years. We really don't have any problems. We're ready to call another pastor." This is **never** the case. The time to grieve the pastor's leaving, the time to assess what has occurred during the past thirty years, the time to look at changes in the make-up of the church and the community, the time to look at the way decisions are made and leadership is exercised, the time to begin to think about this is who we are, these are the gifts we have, and this is where we think we would like to go – is **before** a new pastor is on the scene. The worst thing I have ever heard a search committee say to a candidate was, "Tell us what your program for our church would be?" That is the recipe for an iceberg strike early on!

IT'S TOO COLD AND TOO DARK AND TOO LATE.

Of course, this was not the time of night or the balmy conditions for a pleasant ocean trip in a small boat. But this was not a matter of convenience or comfort; this was a matter of survival. Would anything else be a matter for consideration? The challenge *Choose life!* (Deuteronomy 30:19) seems unnecessary. Would anyone deliberately choose anything that would mean less than life? The answer is all around us and that answer is "Yes."

The Hebrew slaves appear quickly to have forgotten their bitter bondage and harsh treatment in Egypt. After what for us would have been unbelievable acts of Divine intervention, they find themselves facing a literal sea of difficulty and Pharaoh's advancing army over the horizon. The command to go forward was probably the most challenging one Moses ever gave to the people. It remains our basic challenge. "Back to the future" is still the dream for many. If only it were possible! But it's not. Period. The fifties are not coming back and the fastest growing group (the SBNR – the Spiritual but Not Religious) will continue to grow. In its June 5, 2012 edition, the Louisville Courier Journal featured a front page story titled *"A Break from Tradition."* The subtitle is *"More Funerals Focusing on Memories, Rather Than Religion."* A couple of quotes from that article:

> According to the American Religious Identification Survey, conducted by researchers at Trinity College of Hartford, Conn., the proportion of Americans with no religious affiliation nearly doubled to 15 percent between 1990 and 2008, and more than a quarter of U.S. adults expect a non-religious funeral.

> "I always invite people to go to the God of their understanding," and if God isn't part of their belief, then "the place where they connect with the love that binds us all." (Diana Walker, an interfaith minister).

This is the world in which the church now finds itself. In the same issue of the newspaper, one of letters in the Reader's Forum was titled "Advocating Atheism." It contains this sentence: "Religious institutions and the people therein are the best evidence for atheism to date." The writer, no doubt, has his focus on the worst examples of faith but, alas, in this information age, you don't have to wait long or look far to find fodder for his accusation. It's time for those of us who are church and believe in church to prove the writer wrong. We need to be better examples and healthier demonstrations of what being the people of God is all about. My prayer is that this book will aid us in doing just that.

If we are facing forward, we are facing in the right direction. There is no other optional direction. Facing what lies immediately in front of us often means we, too, are confronting a literal sea of difficulty. We see no possibility for getting to the other side and yet there is no reverse in life's transmission gears. Just when we think things cannot get worse, they do. The wicked witch in the *Wizard of Oz* movie speaks for too many of us when, as she melts away, she laments, "What a world! What a world! What a world!" She assumed she could have the world on her terms at the expense of nearly everyone else. The witch's cry parallels the laments the Hebrew people poured out while keeping one eye on Moses and the other on Pharaoh's troops.

The cliché, "It is what it is," cannot be sounded often enough. Whatever our situation, it IS our situation. Whatever shape our world is in, it IS our world. For us, it may seem just as cold, appear just as dark, and seem logically the time for retiring rather than action, just as it did for those on the Titanic. But things were not going to remain as they were. Remaining on board was no longer a safe possibility. A first-time lifeboat journey was the only option. The issues were no longer comfort, convenience, the familiar, and the reassuring. Facing our present reality may not be pleasant but refusing to face it will in the long run be more unpleasant.

AT LEAST WE ARE DOING SOMETHING!

> There was a man who always wore
> A saucepan on his head.
> I asked him what he did it for –
> "I don't know why," he said.
> "It always makes my ears so sore,
> I am a foolish man.
> I think I'll have to take it off,
> And wear a frying pan."[1]

It is much easier to see the nonsense in a children's limerick than it is to see it in our own lives. Our solutions to problem situations in times of high anxiety are often as foolish as substituting

---

1   Iona & Peter Opie, eds., *I Saw Esau* (Cambridge: Candlewick Press, 1992), 25.

a frying pan for a saucepan. (I speak from personal experience.) "Don't just stand there, do something" may not be the best advice we can receive. In C. S. Lewis's *Screwtape Letters*, a piece of advice from senior devil, Screwtape, to his apprentice devil is all too familiar: "The game is to have them all running about with fire extinguishers whenever there is a flood."

When the prophet Jeremiah denounces the people for their idolatry and warns about God's coming judgment, they respond:

> *As for the word that you have spoken to us in the name of the Lord, we are not going to listen to you. Instead, we will do everything that we have vowed, make offerings to the queen of heaven and pour out our libations to her, just as we and our ancestors, our kings and our officials, used to do in the towns of Judah and in the streets of Jerusalem. We used to have plenty of food, and prospered, and saw no misfortune. But from the time we stopped making offerings to the queen of heaven and pouring out libations to her, we have lacked everything and have perished by the sword and famine.* (Jeremiah 44:16-18).

The people choose to do what does not call for repentance (change of direction, mind, and attitude) and transformation. It is something that can be done without drastic change. It has been said that change is the most feared word in our language and yet it remains the most prevalent. I believe that what most of us fear is that we will have to change. The unstated motto continues to be the classic: "Come weal or come woe, my status is quo." It has been said that you cannot live the twilight years by the rules of the morning years. My life in the seventies is not the same as it was in the twenties; to live as though it were is simply the refusal to live with reality. We cannot be the church of the fifties in the new twenty first century.

LAUNCHING THE CAMPAIGN AGAINST DELUSION

Thomas Merton believed one of the primary roles of a good spiritual director to be that of conducting a "ruthless campaign against all forms of delusion arising out of spiritual ambition and self-complacency which aim to establish the ego in spiritual glory."[1] A ruthless campaign against all forms of delusion should be the number one priority in our personal spiritual journeys and in the life and ministry of our congregations. A major delusion that keeps popping up is that the basic requirement is sincerity. "He was so sincere." It is possible to be sincerely wrong. In dealing with the idea that it doesn't matter what one believes as long as one is sincere, I often challenge that idea by saying, "The devil's on the level." While much too simplistic and void of explanation, it usually makes my point. Many sincere people have done great harm to themselves and others. I do not doubt the sincerity of those who participated in the Inquisition or the Salem witch trials. "It is not sincerity, it is Truth which frees us, because it transforms us."[2]

It is easy to spot delusion in its most extreme forms:

> Texas tee shirt describing the Four Stages of Tequila: One drink: I'm rich. Two drinks: I'm good looking. Three drinks: I'm bulletproof. Four drinks: I'm invisible.[3]

If only our own delusions were this quickly recognized! In a recent *Dilbert* cartoon, the boss addresses two of his employees: "I read a book about how to be a great leader and realized I don't do any of those things. I'm surprised that a book with so many errors could get published." It's the repeat of those who could look through Galileo's telescope and not see anything except what they wanted to see. Perhaps Frederick Buechner summarizes it best:

> The temptation is to settle for the lesser good, which is evil enough and maybe a worse one – to settle for niceness and usefulness and busyness instead of for holiness; to settle for plausibility and eloquence instead of for truth.[4]

---

1   James Finley, *Merton's Palace of Nowhere,* 81.
2   Henri de Lubac, quoted in Kathleen Norris, *Acedia & Me* (New York: Riverhead Books, 2008), 143
3   Tad Tuleja, *Quirky Quotations,* 59.
4   Frederick Buechner, *Secrets in the Dark* (San Francisco: HarperOne, 2006), 88.

While I won't go so far as to compare our time like being on board the sinking Titanic (although in many ways it seems just like that), I will say that it cannot be a time for business as usual, for living as usual, for tinkering rather than major overhaul, for courses about new designs in chair arranging. But perhaps these times are just what we need in order to persuade us to do what is necessary.

When Randy Pausch faced the reality of his own mortality, he chose to deliver what he called his "Last Lecture." Even though he lost his battle with cancer on July 25, 2008, his lecture and book are full of inspiration and challenge from one who did not hesitate to deal with his reality. In his book, he tells of a conversation with a student who thought he was doing okay being in the bottom 25 percent of his class. (He actually was dead last.) Among other things, Randy tells him, "I used to be just like you. I was in denial. But I had a professor who showed he cared about me by smacking the truth into my head. And here's what makes me special: I listened."[1]

The times in which we live are smacking the truth into our heads. The only question is, "Will we listen?" This book is the challenge to listen to some truths that demand a hearing if we want to be somewhere other than dead last in our personal, family, church, and community lives. In this introduction, I have hinted at some of the things we will be exploring. These are not all the truths that are out there but these will provide sufficient fodder for reflection and discussion.

Bill Adler's letter from a child to her minister ("I think more people would come to church if you moved it to Disneyland") is not really meant to be contemporary "wisdom" but it is much of contemporary thinking. The adage comes to mind, "A nice place to visit but you wouldn't want to live there." Sadly, many are attempting to do just that. This book is not a call to live in Disneyland. It is the call to live in the real world as it is right now. It is the call to live out our faith and our calling (which we all have) so that when our obituaries and the histories of our churches are written they will be what we always wanted them to be. Mediocrity and

---

1   Randy Pausch, *The Last Lecture* (New York: Hyperion, 2008), 116.

complacency are not the answer. When we look at ourselves and our churches, Dr. Phil's is the necessary question: "And how is that working for you?"

IT'S NOT THE TITANIC, HOWEVER……

I propose to shorten the seven last words of the church ("We've never done it like that before") by three words to: "It can't happen here!" *As it was in the beginning, so it is now, and so it shall ever be* does NOT apply to a local congregation. It is the philosophy of entrenchment and of blinders remaining in place.

Too many congregations do not want to hear modern prophets announce the realities of the present situation. (Note: Biblical prophets were unpopular because their basic calling was to proclaim, "This is how things are." Most pictures of the future were warnings of what would result if current behaviors did not change.) How comfortable are we in listening to these prophetic words :

- "I was shocked that the data also revealed the frustrations of young Christians. Millions of young Christians were also describing Christianity as hypocritical, judgmental, too political, and out of touch with reality."

- "A generation of young Christians believes that the churches in which they were raised are not safe and hospitable places to express doubts. Many feel that they have been offered slick or half-baked answers to their thorny, honest questions, and they are rejecting the "talking heads" and "talking points" they see among the older generations…. Their judgment (is) that the institutional church has failed them."

- "I think this next generation is not just slightly different from the past. I believe they are discontinuously different than anything we have seen before."

- "Christianity is no longer the 'default setting' of American society."

The above quotations come from a book by David Kinnaman (president of the Barna Group) titled *You Lost Me: Why Young Christians Are Leaving Church...and Rethinking Faith*.[1] Even if we do not believe the first two reflect our congregations, all of these observations let us know something about the storm raging outside. I recommend this book for several reasons:

1) It is based on research over a period of four years with thousands of young people ages eighteen to twenty-nine. (This age represents the black hole of church attendance. Kinnaman calls this age segment the "missing in action" from most congregations.)

2) There are many charts throughout the book labeled "In Their Own Words." Every congregation with which I have worked as an interim minister wants desperately to reach this group but most have done little or nothing to engage in meaningful conversation with them. My thesis in attempting to reach young people (or anyone, for that matter) is that we need first of all to listen to them (whether we agree or not is beside the point).

3) A section at the end of the book is called The Research and defines the basic terms used in the studies, has a lengthy discussion on Methodology (persons surveyed, data collected, sample size, and sampling error), and concludes with information about David Kiennaman and the Barna Group (whose research is frequently cited in national publications).

Most will turn immediately to the last chapter in the book, *Fifty Ideas to Find A Generation* which is divided into ideas for (1) everyone; (2) the next generation; (3) parents; (4) pastors, church leaders, and Christian organizations; and (5) supporters of the next generation. Kinnaman acknowledges that every idea will not relate to your particular situation and that the listing is not necessarily an endorsement. These ideas come from many different persons who are attempting to live with new realities.

---

1 David Kinnaman, *You Lost Me* (Grand Rapids: Baker Books, 2011).

You can check out the book by visiting the website www.YouLostMeBook.org.

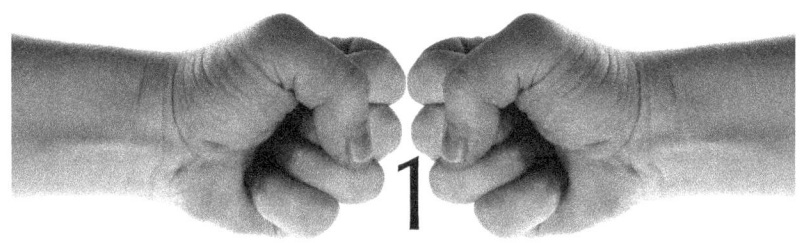

Truth Is only the Beginning of the Journey

THE BIBLICAL WITNESS

>*Teach me you way, O Lord, that I may walk in your truth.* (Psalm 86:11)

>*The sum of your word is truth....* (Psalm 119:160)

>*And the Word became flesh and lived among us, and we have seen his glory, the glory as of a father's only son, full of grace and truth.* (John 1:14)

>*The law was given through Moses; grace and truth came through Jesus Christ.* (John 1:17)

>*"If you continue in my word, you are truly my disciples; and you will know the truth, and the truth will make you free."* (John 8:31-32)

>*"I am the way, and the truth, and the life."* (John 14:6a)

>*"When the Spirit of truth comes, he will guide you into all the truth...."* (John 16:13a)

I was overjoyed to find some of your children walking in the truth, just as we have been commanded by the Father. (2 John 4)

CONTEMPORARY WISDOM

Rules at best are signposts, never hitching posts.[1]

From the cowardice that shrinks from new truths,
From the laziness that is content with half-truths,
And from the arrogance that thinks it knows all truth,
O God of Truth, deliver us. (Ancient Hebrew Prayer).[2]

The temptation is to think that we have finally arrived when actually we are just beginning.[3]

"I FOUND IT!"

The above words are from the bumper sticker that was part of what I believe was, no doubt, a sincere evangelistic effort. It was intended to precipitate the question, "What is it that you have found?" and in return a witness to the faith would follow. My problem with such campaigns is that they are far too simplistic and imply that what ought to be the beginning of a journey is the end of the search.

"Are you saved?" used to be a frequently asked question. This approach to the gospel makes it sound as though salvation is a "transaction," a once and for all decision, a getting it all neatly wrapped up and completed. All that remains is to wait for the Divine summons to glory. Redemption is made to appear to be a simple "once you were out" and "now you are in" and that settles things.

---

1 William Sloane Coffin, *Credo* (Louisville: Westminster John Knox, 2004), 22

2 Henlee Barnette, *A Pilgrimage of Faith* (Macon: Mercer University Press, 2004), 252.

3 Monks of New Skeet, *In the Spirit of Happiness* (Boston: Little, Brown, 1999), 35.

My major complaint in the churches where I was pastor was that far too many of the members considered their salvation a signed, sealed, and delivered matter. The concept of being a community, a community of disciples, that is, and people who were learning together what it means to be God's people in this place for this time was a secondary matter. In an early congregation, one member chastised me with: "You don't need to preach to us. We're already saved. You need to be preaching to the lost."

That request (command!) ignored two problems. The "lost" were nowhere to be found in our services and the person who made the request gave little evidence that his life was marked by the fruit of the Spirit (Galatians 5:22-23). He did not appear to have taken seriously Ephesians 4:15: *But speaking the truth in love, we must grow up in every way into him who is the head, into Christ.* He had "found it" and he just wanted others to "find it." My first thought was that if he had found it, he certainly hadn't done very much with it!

One writer has suggested that evangelism must be understood as "initiation into the kingdom."[1] The first words in the proclamation of both John the Baptist and Jesus are about repentance and the Kingdom (Matthew 3:2; 4:17). The Sermon on the Mount is about how Kingdom citizens live. The most frequently used title for Jesus in the Gospels is "Rabbi" or "Teacher." We are the students and, biblically speaking, school is never out. For some folks, it never seems to have begun. And since motivation is a door locked from the inside, much of my frustration in the pastorate resulted from my refusal to cooperate with the inevitable.

WALKING IN THE TRUTH

The author of 2 John rejoiced that he could find some who were *walking in the truth*. I don't know why I expected it of the majority of congregants. In the average church, only about fifty percent of the membership role is "active." Active is usually interpreted to mean showing any sense of life whatsoever! If someone ever comes or ever gives, that's active. Nominal Christianity has

---

[1] Ronald E. Vallet, *Stewards of the Gospel,* 780.

frequently become normative Christianity. I think the major reason for this is that faith has been interpreted as something you believe. If you believe that Jesus is the Christ, that he died for your sins, and you accept him as your savior, that is it. For some, baptism seals the deal. (There is little sense of baptism being the incorporation into the "body of Christ," the community of faith.)

> The problem with the "Sinner's Prayer" (a prayer, by the way, that you won't find anywhere in the Bible but is widely regarded as the way conversion begins) is that it reduces the human-divine relationship to a onetime transaction rather than a lifetime journey.[1]

Biblically, the earliest Christian confession of faith most likely was: Jesus is Lord. Paul's "plan of salvation" is Romans 10:9-10: *"if you will confess with your lips that JESUS IS LORD and believe in your heart that God raised him from the dead, you will be saved. For one believes with the heart and so is justified, and one confesses with the mouth and so is saved."* In many translations the phrase "Jesus is Lord" is placed in quotation marks indicating its usage as a baptismal confession of faith. In the early church this confession acknowledges that to believe is to announce a new allegiance. It is to make the commitment to the Lordship of Jesus Christ in your life.

It is not incidental that the first disciples were called "Followers of the Way" and in Acts 9:1-2 we find this early designation:

Meanwhile, Saul, still breathing threats and murder against the disciples of the Lord, went to the high priest and asked him for letters to the synagogues at Damascus, so that if he found any who belonged to the Way, men or women, he might bring them bound to Jerusalem.

"Walk this way" is the prelude to a classic comic bit in movies. The one following the person making the request mimics the physical walk of the other. It is meant to bring laughter. The confession "Jesus is Lord" and commitment to be "followers of the Way" is intended to bring transformation. It is intended to bring a new way

---

1 Spencer Burke, *A Heretic's Guide to Eternity* (San Francisco: Jossey-Bass, 2006), 66.

to order one's life, a new way to come at life. The truth discovered in Jesus Christ is meant to provide a new way of walking in the world.

TRUTH COMES BY DEGREES

In looking back over fifty years of pastoral ministry, there is one glaring mistake made by both congregations and pastors that appears to cause the most pain: unrealistic expectations. Many believe that the initial "job description" defines the pastor's role and nothing else is necessary. Many of the most important expectations are assumed already to be understood. "I thought our pastor would" is the most frequently heard complaint. When I began my ministry, I was certain I knew my "job." After all, wasn't this what I had been trained to do? Big question: Did I not understand that this congregation had a history? Why didn't I take the time to hear the answer to the most important question I could have asked them, "Tell me about your life as a congregation?"

Sidebar: One of the first things I do as an intentional interim is to conduct several sessions on the history of the church. We usually begin with a time-line chart on a large wall. Frequently, I will ask members to stand by the year in which they joined; visual presentations are always more striking than simply calling out a year. After encouraging observations, I ask the people to be seated and on small "sticky-note" sheets to record at least one event (without signing) they regard as significant during their time of membership. These are then posted on the time-line chart. The people are then encouraged to take a reading of their "remembered history." Discussion of their reactions are conducted in small groups and then reported out. These significant events are printed and distributed at the next meeting. This process enables many unheard voices to find their place for the first time. It promotes understanding of the perspectives and diversity among the congregation.

Now back to expectations. Not only do expectations need to be fully discussed but they also need frequent updating. Things change, including expectations. In my early pastorates, I did not have enough conversations with the congregation at large. The Search Committee rarely reflects the thinking of every person in the congregation. Sometimes they convey ideas that have never been discussed and approved. In one interim, I found rather heated disagreement over the former pastor's decision to begin an early morning service. He had conveyed to several persons that some on the Search Committee had led him to believe this should be one of his first initiatives. The bottom line was that the congregation had never discussed the nature and purpose of such a service or the advisability of having one. (More about this situation later.)

"I think this is what most people want," is not the same as, "after much discussion, open and free conversation, hearing all points of view, it was the consensus that this would be our course of action." Too many decisions are made in the parking lot after the business meeting. Too many "this is what I really think" discussions are telephone or informal small group discussions outside the decision making structures. This is not the method for healthy communication. I am not talking about an "open mike" meeting in which people are encouraged to "speak their minds." These meetings usually produce disastrous results with the most aggressive (the most vocal) grabbing most of the mike time. The expected result of such gatherings is an increase in the anxiety level of the congregation.

My policy in intentional interims is to conduct "discussions" in a large room with round tables that seat six to eight persons. (This method is used with the time-line chart discussed earlier.) I usually give a brief presentation about our subject for discussion and then have printed questions for each table to discuss. One person acts as recorder/reporter and the group engages in dialogue. I also assign one member of our Transition Team (a small group with whom I work during the interim in planning and coordination) to each table to make certain that one person does not dominate and that the conversation doesn't go off in all directions. The reporter from each table then presents an oral summary of what was discussed. (These summaries will later be printed and made available the following week for all participants.) I lead any general discussion that is necessary and see that the basic rules are in place: only "I" messages may be given (you can only speak for yourself), no attacks are allowed, and only the subject under discussion is permitted. This limits the public speaking to "this is what I believe," and "here is the how and why I see things this way." This type of discussion is intended to promote understanding of issues and of the people holding certain positions. It sounds like a controlled discussion and that is exactly what it is.

If we expect the Spirit to guide us into all truth (John 16:13), there must be free and open flow of information within the congregation. A few privileged "in the know" people is not healthy. (I am not speaking here about confidentiality at certain stages during a search process or of delicate, and often legal, personnel issues.) When people do not know, they begin living on their assumptions – a most disruptive place to set up camp! Clear communication, clear and periodically updated expectations, do not necessarily eliminate conflict; they help prevent the conflict from becoming destructive. Conflict comes with the territory in ALL relationships. In a culture of little genuine conversation and authentic dialogue, the church is the best place I know to begin to model how this is done.

I have found Emily Dickinson's wisdom to be an excellent discussion starter on the nature of helpful conversation and dialogue:

> Tell the truth but tell it slant,
> Success in circuit lies;
> Too bright for mind's infirm intent,
> Is truth's sublime surmise.
> Like lightning to the children eased,
> Through revelation kind;
> The truth must dazzle gradually,
> Or every man be blind.

TRUTH AS A PERSON

Truth in a person and truth as a person is the transforming idea of truth. It is living truth as opposed to static truth. It is easy to quote: *You will know the truth and the truth will make you free* and ignore two things. First of all, that truth is IN the one who said *I am the truth*. Second, the prefix to the idea of truth that sets us free is: *If you CONTINUE in my word, you are truly my DISCIPLES; and you will know the truth, and the truth will set you free* (John 8:31-32, emphasis mine).

This truth is not simply a list of things I believe; it is not truth set in stone but in a person. It is not something I possess, it is something that is to take possession of me. This takes time and effort and constant reexamination.

Learning, and unlearning, can take place only in the absence of defensiveness. When we drop our defenses, we can learn. And we can drop our defenses only when we love and are loved.[1]

Whenever I have been on the defensive, I have gotten into trouble. The stance of defensiveness has nothing to do with the self-differentiation that is so vital to those in positions of leadership. (Much more about this in a later chapter.) A large part of my problem in many of my pastorates was two-fold: first, I was naive enough to believe that it was possible to please almost everybody; second, as with many of those in ministry, I too often fit this description in one of C. S. Lewis' novels: "Mark liked to be liked. There was a good deal of the spaniel in him." I confess that I have a lot of spaniel in me. Both of the above are hazards for the kind of persons who are in the "helping" professions. Of course, this put me in the middle of things and not the people I was supposed to be serving.

We all need to do much unlearning, not because we believe so much that isn't true, but because much of what we hold as truth is partial truth. There are always larger dimensions and greater truths that must be allowed to stand beside our understandings. Getting on the defensive shuts the windows to the wind of the Spirit. I recall the day two men came into my office with the accusation that I did not support the Sunday School. Immediately, I shifted to the defensive and before I knew it was hyperventilating! That is the only time I have ever had such an experience and I'm convinced it was the result of going into hyper-defense. Their charge was not true and they had an agenda but my first response should have been

---
1   William Sloane Coffin, *Credo*, 26.

In Changing Times

the question, "What exactly is it you think I ought to be doing in relation to our Sunday School." With other issues, on my better days I would say, "This is how I see it, now tell me what your take on this matter is."

> The worst thing we can do with a dilemma is to resolve it prematurely because we haven't the courage to live with uncertainty.[1]

Too often I refused to live with the anxiety that is always a part of any relational system – including the church. Anxiety is a part of life. The goal is to keep the anxiety at a "normal" level and make certain it is based on reality. I rephrase, "If you can't stand the heat stay out of the kitchen," to "If you can't tolerate a little anxiety, stay out of the pastorate." It comes with the territory. Why didn't I know that at the beginning?

THE NEED FOR COMPASSION AND RESPECT

It is easy to forget the nature of truth and the embodiment of that truth in the one who said that his most important command to us is that we love one another as he has loved us (John 15:12). In defense of treasured truths (interpretations of those truths), it is so easy to violate the central teachings of the one who we believe gave us those truths. It is so easy to fail to reflect the compassion and respect that were a part of his earthly ministry and are to mark us as his followers continuing his ministry. This has little to do with "putting up with people" or "tolerating" other points of view. It seems to me this demands that we see every person we met as a human being created in the image of God. It demands that we respect the points of view of others and give "learning listening" to the recitation of those viewpoints. (This does not mean we condone destructive agendas.) Respectful listening, especially to opposing ideas, is one of the best pastoral things I ever did.

Luther and Zwingli disagreed over Jesus' statement *This is my body*. Whether the Eucharist in Matthew 26:26 meant that the bread was "identical" with his body or "symbolized" his body. No

---
1 Ibid, 125.

doctrine of inerrancy could have settled the issue, which became the dividing line between historical Lutheranism and the Reformed tradition.[1]

What followed this controversy was Zwingli's refusal to shake hands with Luther and the refusal to accept one another as brothers in Christ in spite of this disagreement. The larger truth that might have enabled that handshake is Paul's declaration in Colossians 1:27: *...the riches of the glory of this mystery which is Christ in you, the hope of glory.* What difference will it make if we can see the Christ in all of those who confess *Jesus is Lord*? What difference will it make if we can see this living truth in all our brothers and sisters?

I read recently of a pastor who decided to do something to remind his congregation who they are. He noted that in other traditions, the minister enters the sanctuary and bows toward the altar. He decided each Sunday to begin the service by bowing to the congregation. "After all," he said, "are they not the body of Christ?" *"You are the body of Christ and individual members of it"* (1 Corinthians 12:27), Paul reminded the church at Corinth. I hardly ever hear this mentioned when one is attempting to give a definition of the church. This is the New Testament definition that ought to be revived for the sake of a truth that is the place to begin in understanding ourselves and our relationship to those who gather with us in the buildings we have mislabeled churches. They only house the church; we are the church; we are the body of Christ. Christ in us is the hope of glory. The truth, the living truth, abides in us. How would this truth change the way we begin to see one another?

In writing about Advent, Douglas John Hall notes:

> The whole truth cannot be put into words, and it need not be. The whole truth is there only in the one who said, "I am the truth." In relation to this one Word, all our words are relative – mixtures of truth and error, fact and fantasy, myth and longing.[2]

---

1 Carl Raschke, *The Next Reformation* (Grand Rapids: Baker Academic, 2004), 131.
2 Douglas John Hall, *Thinking the Faith* (Minneapolis: Augsburg, 1989), 196.

QUESTIONS FOR REFLECTION AND DISCUSSION

1. On a scale of one to ten, how much resistance to change is there in your congregation?

2. What about our present world and culture would have appeared unthinkable a generation ago?

3. Why do you believe the biblical prophets got into so much trouble?

4. Why are cosmetic changes so much easier than basic changes?

5. What has most alarmed your congregation about the changing face of the present "church-world"?

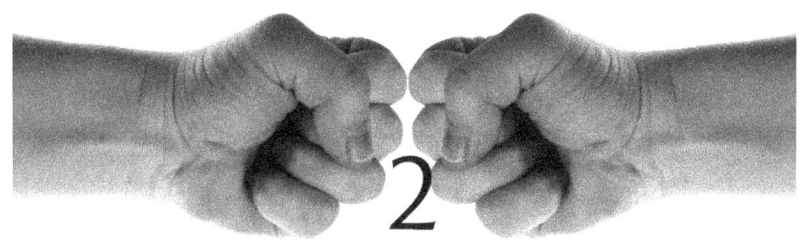

The Big Picture Provides Perspective

THE BIBLICAL WITNESS

> *The steadfast love of the Lord never ceases, his mercies never come to any end; they are new every morning; great is your faithfulness.* (Lamentations 3:22-23)

> *Instead, strive for his kingdom, and these things will be given to you as well.* (Luke 12:31)

> *And I will show you a more excellent way .... And now faith, hope, and love abide, these three; and the greatest of these is love. Pursue love.* (1 Corinthians 12:31, 13:13, 14:1a)

> *But Jesus has now obtained a more excellent ministry, and to that degree he is the mediator of a better covenant, which has been enacted through better promises.* (Hebrews 8:6)

CONTEMPORARY WISDOM

> The lack of a larger perspective hobbles the mind...[1]

---

1   Sven Birkets, *The Gutenberg Elegies* (New York Fawcett Combine, 1994), 73.

No piece of information is processed in isolation.[1]

The explosion of data…and the collapse of what the theorists call the "master narrative" has all but destroyed the premise of understandability. Inundated by perspectives, by lateral vistas of information that stretch endlessly in every direction, we no longer accept the possibility of assembling a complete picture. Instead of carrying on the ancient project of philosophy – attempting to discover the "truth" of things – we direct our energies to managing information.[2]

The message in the Rubik's Cube: Any solution has to be a total solution, acknowledging every facet of life. In a word, wholeness.[3]

The Sermon on the Mount is not a program for legislative and social reform. It is a description of a lifestyle by which we will know those who have accepted God's kingdom; a lifestyle which flows, albeit not easily, from the joy and happiness and love which one experiences when one has decisively responded to the invitation to the wedding feast.[4]

WHEN DO YOU HAVE ENOUGH INFORMATION?

In my early pastorates, the first thing I attempted to do was to gather as many statistics as possible. Statistics about the congregation's life over the past several years, numbers relating to attendance and budgets, and data about the neighborhood in which the church was located. I was usually given the most recent "Long Range Plan" or, infrequently, a self-study. Armed with this information I felt I could come to some understanding of what kind of a church this was and where it was headed. I couldn't have been more mistaken.

---

1 David Brooks, *The Social Animal* (New York: Random House, 2011), 181.
2 Sven Birkets, *The Gutenberg Elegies*, 75.
3 Rick Fields, *Chop Wood Carry Water*, 212.
4 Andrew Greeley, *Myths of Religion* (New York: Warner Books, 1989), 94.

While I had a written history of the congregation in hand, I did not have their stories. I did not have the things that had really shaped the life and ministry of the people. I did not have any sense of how people had experienced the things that had occurred and how they really felt about their past, present, or future. Not only did I not see the big picture, I was not aware that I needed to. What a mistake!

When the big picture is ignored there is little understanding about the conflict that quickly emerges. In life, it is hardly ever true that "one size fits all" and when it comes to churches it is never true that one picture fits all. Each church has its unique history, its unique story. No book can tell you "this is what churches are like" because no two churches are alike. It is only the naive pastor who begins his work with the assumption that he knows what the congregation needs and he knows exactly how to "fix" things.

I discovered that the best way to begin a pastorate was to make no changes for at least six months to a year and spend the initial months of ministry in simply getting to know the congregation. After all, I didn't know them, and they didn't know me. Resumes, biographical data sheets, and church profiles are only the introductory materials in the matter of learning about each other. Bringing an agenda to a church you don't know is a sure-fire recipe for disaster. Getting to know a congregation, listening to the individual and family stories, and getting the big picture, takes time.

IMPORTANCE OF THE LARGER VIEW

In a workshop on *Leadership and Anxiety in the Church*, Richard Blackburn maintained that the pastor needs to get the high stadium view, not one from the bleachers on the fifty yard line. He reminded us that we need to ask questions and avoid interpretation or giving answers. A major emphasis was what I know to be fact: diagnosis polarizes! The only way to get the high stadium view is to refrain from the great pastoral temptation: "Let me tell you what we need to do." Immediately two groups emerge: those who agree with you and those who don't. Also, you have given your diagnosis and not allowed a shared answer to come from people who have given the matter much thought in listening and dialogue.

It's not easy to keep to the questions because so often the answers seem all too obvious! Problem: they are all too obvious to the uninformed observer. Later, we will talk about the need to have someone around who can keep asking us the right questions but for now it is enough to say that almost always the questions are more important than answers coming from the pastor. When I was quick to give the "answer," the only thing I really learned was how quickly I could put people on the defensive and generate conflict. I wanted to ask, "What's going on here? "But if I had approached things differently, it would have been an unnecessary question.

One of the reasons I always begin an interim pastorate with sessions on the history of the congregation (using the time line discussed in the last chapter) is that I need to get the bigger picture before we can begin to address the "problems" that have been shared with me by the search committee. My wife's experience as a marriage and family therapist quickly taught her that the stated problem that brings couples into counseling is most often not the real problem. It is usually a symptom of the real problem. So it is with churches. The thing that "needs to be dealt with" is usually only the beginning of the things that need to be dealt with. The identified issues are usually not the real issues.

LINEAR THINKING AS OPPOSED TO SYSTEMS THINKING

The usual approach to things is what is called the linear approach. It is the simple cause and effect approach. Something is wrong, something has caused this, we'll find out what (who) has caused this. An illustration given by Richard Blackburn in his *Leadership and Anxiety in the Church* workshop was a comment made by a disgruntled parishioner about the deadness of his church: "You can't have fire in the pews if you have ice in the pulpit." Meaning: "The pastor is the problem in our church." Blackburn noted that in times of high anxiety we are wired to see things in linear fashion.

Unfortunately, this promotes the blame game as in his illustration. If only things were that simple!

In the systems approach, everything is taken into account because every part of a system has an impact on every other part of the system. Power structures and struggles, past hurts and injustices, relationships with former pastors, present relationships in families, struggles that people are presently having with jobs, bosses, budgets, health, in-laws, et cetera. **all** are part of the system. We never simply bring ourselves to any situation, we bring all of our relationships. We bring everything of which we are a part.

Sometimes I have discovered (a little too late) that I reminded someone of a former pastor who was quite dictatorial; they never told me this but related to me as if I was this other person. This is usually done on an unconscious level, which makes it all the more destructive. I have often wondered just how many people were involved in the relationship I was having with a person when things seemed to go from bad to worse. Simply asking, "What's going on here?" was not going to generate sufficient information. Patiently asking questions and really listening to words and pauses was the only approach to a more positive relationship.

Only other people can tell you where they are coming from, how they see things, how they hear what you are saying, and how they feel about what is going on. We don't know these things unless others tell us. Not much is discovered or resolved when linear thinking takes charge. I made the following notes as Blackburn compared the linear, cause-effect model with the systems model:

In the linear model the focus is on the individual parts, behavior is seen as unidirectional, events are seen in isolation, patterns go unobserved, and the patterns of the past are repeated. In the systems model: the focus is on the whole system, behavior is seen as mutually influenced, events are seen as interrelated, patterns are identified, and the aim is the work at changing unhealthy patterns.

A LOT OF BAGGAGE IS NEVER UNPACKED

One minister was quoted as saying, "The clergy collar is the screen on which parishioners show home movies." We used to call this "projection" but not quite in such literal terms! Why didn't I know this early on? Why don't people in congregations recognize this? We all do it many times and we don't limit our showings to a clergy collar. It's the way all relationships work and the more we discover this happening the better our relationships will be.

I remember in one church receiving a scathing letter from a member of the congregation. It was hand written, several pages in length, and filled with biblical quotes. It was difficult to get the final message except that this person was most unhappy with me and my approach. It was unsigned. In a couple of weeks I received another weighty tome with basically the same message. I then did something that I had never done (and haven't done since). The financial secretary was a trusted member of the staff and I asked her to check the pledge cards and see if she could match the writing in these letters with a signature. She found the match.

The following Sunday as soon as I looked out at the congregation I spotted the letter writer. She was seated close to the front with her usual somber expression. But there was not a hint of anger or resentment present in me as I glanced her way because I knew something about her story. She had several siblings. Many years earlier there had been a discussion about the best way to take care of their aging, widowed mother. By some method, it was decided that this woman would abandon her career and be the caregiver. The family had more than sufficient funds to pay her and all expenses. For years, this woman had practically been homebound as the care for her mother became 24/7 and the family was adamantly opposed to a nursing home. A sense of isolation, despair, and a note of understandable self-pity had been evident in her letters. I wondered how I would feel in her circumstances.

I never confronted her (you **never** do that) but used the opportunities that came to be her pastor. Her situation never changed but what changed was my attitude and the way I related to her. Knowing her story made all the difference. Of course, she brought her story with her to church; she couldn't leave it at home. None of us can! The best we can do is to be aware of what is going on in our system – to attempt to discover the baggage we are carrying

In Changing Times 33

around with us. The discovering and the unpacking is the work of a lifetime. (Perhaps the work of eternity; this may be what a large portion of the next life is all about).

LET'S NOT GET DEADLY SERIOUS ABOUT THIS

> Maybe I had expected too much. I had been in love with China since the first time I went there in 1980, thinking I might be able to shoot a sequel to *The Four Seasons*. I loved the people, and I tried to teach myself the language, tripping over the tones, the way I had in glee club as a boy. In Mandarin, if you get one of four musical tones wrong, the word means something else. I took my movie to a group of filmmakers and told them in my weirdest Chinese, "I'm very happy to show you my film: *Four Seasons*." I had the words right, but not the tones. What they heard me say was: "I'm very happy to show you my film: *Dead Chicken*."[1]

The two lessons for pastor and congregation to be gained from this excerpt from a delightful book are basic to my work as an intentional interim pastor. The first is that nothing takes the place of a little bit of humor when dealing with anxiety ridden situations. In systems it is called maintaining a sense of playfulness. Taking oneself deadly serious can indeed be deadly. It is obvious that Alan Alda got a lot of laughs out of his failed attempt to communicate.

Nothing defuses a situation like the refusal to take oneself too seriously. The entire atmosphere is often transformed by recognition of just how funny we are in our attempts to deal with serious matters. It's not just the pastor who can make this contribution. After about six months in a new pastorate, I had a challenging question at a deacon's meeting. The group was large and impressive in both occupation and skills. After giving a few brief remarks, I asked if there were any questions. "After your first few months with us, what are some of your impressions?" I paused for a moment and said, "Well, I have observed that we have a lot of chiefs and

---

1 Alan Alda, *Things I Overheard While Talking To Myself* (New York: Random House, 2008), 66-67.

very few Indians." The follow-up question came: "Would you mind pointing out the Indians?" Laughter filled the room and it took a while for me to regain my composure. We then discussed the degree and quality of excellent leadership the church possessed. There were many CEOs in the deacon body and in the congregation and that was a great asset. It was also a genuine challenge for the pastor. But, once again, humor saved the day.

The other lesson from the Alda story is that if you have the right words but not the tone you will communicate something quite different from what you intended. I will enlarge this by saying we need to be aware of the tone of things, the texture of things, the feel of things, the surrounding atmosphere, the way things are put together. "Just the facts" will never do. The facts always have to be in context – in the largest context we can discover. With the explosion of data we have lost the master narrative. We live in a culture with an information explosion that does not translate into the bigger picture. If anything, it seems to obscure our vision.

I quoted Andrew Greeley in the "Contemporary Wisdom" section because it is what I believe to be one of the missing ingredients in the Christian faith. I have given this assignment in Bible studies: "Read the Sermon on the Mount (Matthew 5 – 7). Then close your Bible and ask, 'What kind of person is described in this sermon?'" A similar question is asked after an overview of the Bible study: "What kind of a God is described in this book and what is it he expects of us?"

I don't see how you can understand anything until you get the big picture. The brief biblical witness section speaks about the covenant-making, promise-making God of Scripture who is faithful to his promises and abounding in mercy and grace. The new covenant established in Jesus Christ is all about the reign of God in our lives that has the priority of love, the kind of love we have received from him. With this kind of a broad understanding, many of our questions either are answered or we find them no longer necessary.

Getting the big picture mandates that we abandon linear thinking and try to envision all the relationships, levels of communications, and influences that are at work in our church.

QUESTIONS FOR REFLECTION AND DISCUSSION

1. When do we have enough information? What do we do with the information when we have it?

2. How do you explain the differences between linear thinking as opposed to systems thinking?

3. Why does so much baggage remain unpacked in our congregations?

4. How have you found humor to be a helpful asset in difficult/tense life and church situations?

5. How would you describe the big picture of what we are about as congregations?

Control Is in Short Supply

THE BIBLICAL WITNESS

> *When Esau was forty years old, he married Judith daughter of Beeri the Hittite, and Basemath daughter of Elon the Hittite; and they made life bitter for Isaac and Rebekah.* (Genesis 26:34-35)

> *"The Lord watch between you and me, when we are absent from one another...."* (Genesis 31:49)

> *My times are in your hand....* (Psalm 31:15a)

CONTEMPORARY WISDOM

> The Heisenberg Uncertainty Principle has been reduced, by now, to an almost commonplace tidbit of everyday conversation... "uncertainty" became the only fact that could be accepted as fact, not only in the popular mind, but also in large segments of the academic mind as well.[1]

---

1 Phyllis Tickle, *The Great Emergence* (Grand Rapids: Baker Books, 2008), 79.

And here is the conundrum for a results-oriented, American can-do mentality: the only control the planter has is in the act of planting.[1]

Much of the time, we cannot control what happens to us. But we can always control how we respond to what happens to us.[2]

Parkinson's and alcohol took a sledgehammer to any illusions I may have had that I was in control.[3]

THE MOST COMMONLY HELD ILLUSION

I have written in an earlier book about the bedrock on which biblical ministry in the church must always be based: we are responsible for input, not outcome. We can manage only what we will do in given situations; we cannot superintend the results. (Question: Why does this sound like heresy when it is definitely biblical?) Nothing provides more frustration (and ultimately despair) than attempting to control that which does not belong to us but to God.

"*I planted, Apollos watered, but God gave the growth*" (1 Corinthians 3:6). Paul clearly announces the part of ministry that belongs to him and Apollos and the part that is the exclusively God's domain. Evidently, most church leaders have not read this verse of Scripture because in every one of my pastorates the first announced "goal" was growth. This is not a goal, this is an outcome, an outcome that belongs to God and not to us. If growth becomes the driving engine in the life of a congregation, the temptation is to do whatever is necessary to bring it about, even some things that "bend" the gospel.

From the business world and a book titled *The Heart of a Leader* come two quotes that apply to pastoral and lay leadership in the church. Both of these quotes make good ice-breakers for meetings:

---

1 Krista Tippett, *Speaking of Faith* (New York: Penguin Books, 2008), 58.
2 Harold Kushner, *The Lord Is My Shepherd* (New York: Alfred A. Knopf, 2003), 9.
3 Michael J. Fox, *Always Looking Up* (New York: Hyperion, 2009), 201.

> Nice guys may appear to finish last, but usually they are running in a different race. (Compare this with John 18:36: "My kingdom is not from this world.")[1]

> Managing only for profit (you can substitute the word growth) is like playing tennis with your eye on the scoreboard and not on the ball.[2]

"We want to call a pastor who will enable us to grow," is practically the first word that comes from a search committee. This I fully understand. Most churches are either in the plateau or declining mode. "The future looks none too bright unless we can attract some younger families. In twenty years few of us will be left, then what will happen?" The underlying thesis is the belief that it is possible to control the future of the congregation, to ensure its survival. "My times are in your hand" (Psalm 31:15a) is true not only for our individual lives but for the life of our church as well.

IT'S JUST ONE UNCERTAIN THING AFTER ANOTHER

The Old Testament contains many warnings about consulting wizards and fortune tellers. Do not turn to mediums and wizards; do not seek them out, to be defiled by them: I am the Lord your God (Leviticus 19:31). Interpreting this passage is not difficult. If the people consulted wizards and mediums it signaled that they were no longer putting their trust in the God who called them into covenant relationship. They no longer were putting their faith in him for their future. They no longer were demonstrating confidence in God's ability to take care of what lay ahead. Also, they wanted to know what was coming. Couldn't we all be better prepared if we had a little advance warning?

In the Sermon on the Mount, Jesus instructs his disciples not to worry about the necessities of life (food, water, clothing, housing) but to have faith that God will provide (Matthew 6:25-33). Then he shocked them (and us) with: *"So do not worry about tomorrow, for tomorrow will bring worries of its own. Today's trouble is*

---

1 Ken Blanchard, *The Heart of A Leader* (Tulsa: Honor Books, 1999), 6.
2 Ibid, 40.

enough for today" (verse 34). This is a tough verse to "explain" for those who believe that the Christian faith will eliminate trouble, problems, difficulties, etc. Not only is today packed with challenges, but tomorrow will bring new troubles! *You do not even know what tomorrow will bring* (James 4:14a) is not a popular sermon text. It's the stark reminder that we cannot control the future. We cannot manage outcomes.

Michael J. Fox has written at least two books about his continuing battle with Parkinson's. In the Contemporary Wisdom quote, he confesses that Parkinson's and his alcohol addiction took a sledgehammer to any illusions he had about being in control. Hopefully, it will not take such a drastic sledgehammer to bring us to one of life's basics. "It's all about control" is never spoken as a compliment. We all understand how quickly those who seek control can distort and destroy much of what they intend to make better.

The families in the book of Genesis do not give us many examples of "family values" we want to emulate. (There are family squabbles galore and at least two announced death threats by brothers against Jacob and Joseph.) They do let us know that the Bible is about real people and that life has not changed very much. The announcement that Esau's wives made life bitter for Isaac and Rebekah is not a surprise to many who simply shake their heads and say, "We know all about that!" Would a workshop on "How to Have a Happy Family" have solved that problem? To placate his father, Esau later marries one of Ishmael's daughters, thus uniting one unblessed son into the family of another unblessed son.

The quote from Genesis 31:49, *The Lord watch between you and me when we are absent from one another*, is very inspiring as long as it is taken out of context. The reality is quite different. Laban has just overtaken his son-in-law, Jacob, who has fled with his daughters and gains from twenty years of service. After a session of mutual complaints, Laban and Jacob make a covenant with one another. The symbol of their commitment is a heap of stones over which Laban utters the words we rightly read: "I know the kind of trickster you are. I can't keep my eye on you now that you are leaving and taking my Rachel and Leah with you. So I'm charging God to keep his eye on you while I'm not there to do it!" You never know what family members might be up to!

We are reminded in the first book of the Bible of the difficulty and complexity of family relationships; in the New Testament letters we are reminded of the difficulty and complexity of church family relationships. In relationships as well as life it is one uncertain thing after another. Parents learn all too slowly and painfully how impossible it is to "control" their children. (Billy Sunday's own children were not converted!)[1] Pastors learn all too slowly and painfully how impossible it is to "control" the members of their congregation. But is control what we are really supposed to be about in family and in church? A one word answer: "No."

TAKING ANOTHER LOOK

In writing about a recent surgery, Tom Parks said:

> I was real calm about the operation. 'Til I realized what I was doing. I'm lying there naked. On a table in front of people I don't know. And they have knives. What's wrong with this picture?"[2]

The above quote is from a book titled *The Courage to Laugh*. It's in a chapter called "What's So Funny About Haspitals?" ("Hospitals" is deliberately misspelled.) The focus is on the value of humor in dealing with the serious matters of health. (We will shortly apply this to church situations where people often forget the value of a smile or good laugh in the face of things not working as they should – as we expected.) A few snippets from *The Courage to Laugh*:

> A. In a cartoon, a man has just donned one of those notorious hospital gowns. The caption reads: "Now I know why they call it I.C.U."[3]

---

1   Douglas Weaver, ed., *From Our Christian Heritage* (Macon: Smyth & Helwys, 1997), 264.
2   Allen Klein, *The Courage To Laugh* (New York: Jeremy P. Tarcher/Putnam, 1998), 55.
3   Ibid, 55.

B. You no longer die in the hospital, you merely experience "negative patient outcome."[1]
C. "It is the patient's responsibility to lighten up a hospital experience." Norman Cousins.[2]
D. Mr. Barnes was scheduled for abdominal surgery. He arrived in the operating room grinning from ear to ear. Soon after the staff began preparing him for surgery, they started to laugh. On his stomach they found a sticker requesting, "Hey, Doc, while you're in there could you check the oil?" (From an article entitled "Jest for Your Health.")[3]
E. "When a situation becomes really awful, I get silly and laugh, make it absurd. The laughter helps me convince myself, 'I can get through this.'" Joan Rivers from her book *Still Talking*.[4]

Some probably think I push this too far, but I am convinced that appropriate humor can often break the tension and bring a sense of relief to an anxiety laden situation. To be able to see ourselves in our full humanity, to at least smile at our foibles and missteps, is to be able to step outside our present dilemma for a few moments. It's our needed "time out." Tears are known as a unifying experience but so is laughter. There is nothing like hearty laughter to give people a new way to look at themselves and each other. The more serious the situation, the more we need laughter. If your congregation does not know how to laugh together (or at least smile), I probably would not be of much assistance as your intentional interim.

Art Linkletter hosted a radio and TV show called *People Are Funny*. They are! We are! In everyday life and in church. Question: Where did the idea originate that people are different when they gather at church than they are in every other relationship? What makes us think that when we gather as God's saints (Paul's desig-

---

1 Ibid, 61.
2 Ibid, 63.
3 Ibid, 64.
4 Ibid, 65.

nation for us!) that we leave our humanity at home? To see and acknowledge just how funny we can be is one of the most therapeutic things I know. I repeat: whenever I have taken myself too seriously I have gotten into a lot of trouble.

A good rule for every congregation in conflict: Lighten up!

THE BOTTOM LINE

The bottom line for us individually and as a church is to be faithful to the calling that comes to us and then to trust God for whatever happens. In another book, I called this "Mastering the Art of Letting Go." It is not only the key to the spiritual life, it is the key to church life. In my interim pastorates, I major on two questions: "What are the gifts of your congregation? With these gifts (strengths) in mind, what do you believe God is calling you to do at this time in this place?"

For all of us the bottom line is: we do what we believe we are called to do with the gifts we have under the circumstances that prevail – and then we let it go. We have done all we can do. My great rule of thumb is: We are in charge of input, not outcome.

We are able to let go to the extent that we are able to trust God for whatever outcome there is. One of the best gifts we can ever give ourselves in response to the question, "Did it turn out the way you expected?" is to be able to say, "It didn't have to." We don't necessarily know the best outcomes anyway. When we are committed to a certain outcome, strange things can happen. The following is true:

> A company purchased laptop computers for employees to use while traveling. Fearing they might be stolen, the managers came up with a clever solution: permanently attach the laptop computers to the employees' desks.[1]

Much of our control looks like this when viewed from a distance. Much of what I have seen in a similar church situation has made me want to echo, "If I hadn't laughed, I would have cried."

---

1   Scott Adams, *The Dilbert Principle* (New York: HarperCollins, 1996), 1.

Although Clifford Kuhn was not writing for churches, much of what he has to say is applicable. He gives "Leadership Strategies" that are intended to strengthen and sustain a fun atmosphere. I won't guarantee a fun atmosphere but I think they are excellent strategies for church leaders.[1]

1. Listen very carefully.

2. Stay focused, but remain flexible.

3. Be willing to laugh at yourself.

4. Keep expecting the unexpected.

5. Welcome mistakes.

6. Act and interact.

7. Build in relevance to the larger community.

8. Celebrate everything.

WHERE PASTORS AND CHURCH LEADERS NEED TO MAJOR ON CONTROL

This reminder should be posted where we can see it every day: "Much of the time, we cannot control what happens to us. But we can always control how we respond to what happens to us."[2] As an intentional interim, we are instructed to be above all else a "non-anxious presence" in the congregation. We cannot manage anyone else's actions or responses but we can take charge of our own. I cannot choose my feelings but I can choose my actions. (That often means pausing between my initial feelings and the way I decide to respond. It often involves counting to much more than ten!)

I will never forget the wise counsel of John Powell in his workshop with over five hundred ministers. It is so easy to react with, "You make me so angry!" Or "I get so upset when you say that (or

---

1 Clifford Kuhn, *The Fun Factor* (Louisville: Minerva Books, 2002), 115-125.
2 Harold Kushner, *The Lord Is My Shepherd*, 9.

do that)!" He gave us the strategy he used to maintain the correct perspective in such situations. "No one has the ability to 'make' me angry unless I choose to allow them to do so. Whenever I find myself beginning to respond in anger, I ask, 'What is in me that has prompted me to respond in this way?'" The focus was shifted from the other person to himself. "What is in me that precipitates such reactions?" is an ongoing question with ongoing discoveries.

In systems thinking we call this "self-differentiation." In his workshop lecture, Richard Blackburn stressed the need to focus on self and not others and to define ourselves out of our principles, values, and beliefs. These beliefs are to be calmly stated, not shouted as commandments received from the Almighty. One of the most important things he said was, "If you can control your emotional response, you can interrupt a chain reaction."

Self-differentiated leadership never comes as a reactive response. It is never fueled by anger. Every pastor and church leader should take note of Blackburn's dictum: "You do not insist that others change!" My take on that is, you do not insist that others allow you to control them. When you do not insist that others change, when they know you are not out to control them, the defensive walls begin to come down making possible open discussion and genuine dialogue.

A book I recommend as a must for every person in any position of leadership is Edwin Friedman's *A Failure of Nerve*. He summarizes much of what he has to say about leadership in a chart comparing poorly differentiated leadership with well-differentiated leadership. Here is a portion of that chart:[1]

---

[1] Edwin Friedman, *A Failure of Nerve* (New York: Seabury Books, 2007), 231.

LEADERSHIP	
POORLY DIFFERENTIATED	WELL-DIFFERENTIATED
Focuses on pathology	Focuses on strength
Works with symptomatic people	Works with motivated people
Betters the condition	Matures the system
Seeks symptomatic relief	Seeks enduring change
Is concerned to give insight	Is concerned to define self (takes stands)
Diagnoses others	Looks at one's own stuck-ness
Is quick to quit difficult situations	Is challenged by difficult situations
Is made anxious by reactivity	Recognizes that reactivity and sabotage are evidence of one's effectiveness
Sees problems as the cause of anxiety	Sees problems as the focus of preexisting anxiety
Adapts toward the weak	Adapts toward strength
Focuses empathically on helpless victims	Has a challenging attitude that encourages responsibility
Is more likely to create dependent relationships	Is more likely to create dependent relationships

You need to read the book for a full explanation of these ideas, but Friedman gives this brief summary of what he means by the leader's own self-differentiation:

> I mean his or her capacity to be a non-anxious presence, a challenging presence, a well-defined presence, and a paradoxical presence. Differentiation is not about being coercive, manipulative, reactive, pursuing, or invasive, but being rooted

In Changing Times

in the leader's own sense of self rather than focused on that of his or her followers.[1]

QUESTIONS FOR REFLECTION AND DISCUSSION

1. How difficult is it to confess (and believe) that we are in charge of input and not results?

2. Do you believe that church growth is an outcome and not a goal? What difference does it make?

3. What can we learn about the difficulty and complexity of family (and church) relationships from the book of Genesis?

4. What do you think of Clifford Kuhn's leadership strategies?

5. How important is self-differentiated leadership? Do you agree with Edwin Friedman's comparison chart?

---

1   Ibid, 230.

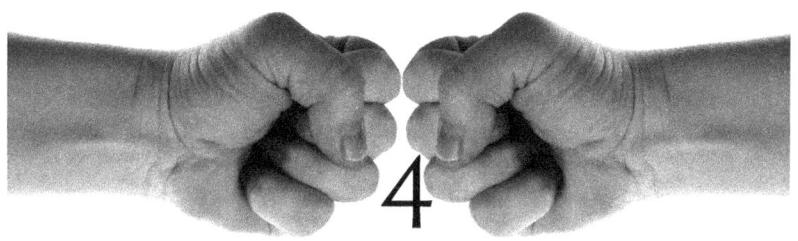

BELIEFS AND ATTITUDES SHAPE OUR WORLD

THE BIBLICAL WITNESS

For as he thinks in his heart, so is he. (Proverbs 23:7, KJV)

Keep your heart with all vigilance, for from it flow the springs of life. (Proverbs 4:23)

We love because he first loved us. (I John 4:19)

CONTEMPORARY WISDOM

Surprisingly few people take time to identify the thoughts behind their emotions....Learning to identify the thoughts associated with the day's first moods, energy shifts, and the emotions is particularly useful within the over purpose of this book (*The Little Book of Letting Go*).[1]

Our beliefs are so powerful that they color our entire world. We literally see what we believe.[2]

---

1   Hugh Prather, *The Little Book of Letting Go* (New York: MJF Books, 2000), 102.
2   Ibid, 195.

A change of heart is always a change of mind.[1]

"That which dominates our imagination and our thoughts will determine our life and character."[2]

There is no such thing as non-contextual human thought, including theological thought.[3]

Wisdom is not the gathering of more facts and information, as if that would eventually coalesce into truth. Wisdom is a different way of seeing and knowing those ten thousand things.[4]

IT'S AN INSIDE JOB

When I became pastor of a congregation new to me, I should have looked out that first Sunday and said: "Not only are we probably not all on the same page, most of us are not even reading from the same book." What brought all of us to that moment is the total context of our lives and no single "personality inventory" can ever tell us "this is who we are and this is why we come at things as we do." The things that have shaped us are manifold and complex and are now all inside us waiting to take over.

My first job, however, is not to find out where these people are coming from but to attempt to discover where I'm coming from. I am amazed at how naive I was about my own presuppositions, assumptions, foregone conclusions, and the influences that were responsible for who and where I was. Until I begin to understand myself, how can I possibly begin to understand others? There is a sense in which we will always remain a mystery to ourselves but we certainly owe it to ourselves to try to become less of a mystery.

---

1   Richard Rohr, *The Naked Now* (New York: Crossroad Publishing, 2009), 34.
2   Attributed to Ralph Waldo Emerson.
3   John Douglas Hall, *Thinking the Faith*, 76.
4   Richard Rohr, *The Naked Now*, 59.

One of the first things my wife did with the couples who came to her for counseling was to assist them in drawing up a genogram. This was more than the picture of a family tree; it provided a little insight into the contexts that had shaped the relationships in their families. Knowing the rural background of both of my grandparents, the harsh realities of tenant farming, the depression that robbed my parents of the opportunity to complete their educations, and the ethical values that shaped their lives, gave me some understanding of how I came to see many things.

"We do not see things as they are; we see things as we are" is an observation made by many. I remember someone writing: "I have a point of view, you have a point of view, only God has view." Only God sees things as they are. The rest of us see through the lenses of all that we have experienced. My favorite mythical book title of all times is: *An Unbiased Account of the Civil War from the Southern Viewpoint*. Could it be anything else? Even the best history writing has the element of interpretation. Nobody can give "just the facts." "Fair and balanced" is a worthy goal but can never be a total achievement.

YOU CAN'T CHANGE YOUR IQ BUT YOU CAN CHANGE YOUR EQ

The real problem, of course, is that we often remain unaware of the things deep within us that bring the feelings and reactions that take control of our lives. I have personally found the concept of "emotional intelligence" a valuable tool for not only increasing awareness of what goes on in that interior darkroom but for learning a few skills about managing my responses a little better. (Notice the qualifying adjectives!).

One of my best Half-Price Bookstore finds is *The Emotional Intelligence Quick Book* by Travis Bradberry and Jean Greaves. I recommend this for pastors and church leaders who want a brief, but solid, overview of the subject. I am going to mine for you some of the treasures I found in this book.

William James' most famous quote is: "Human beings, by changing the inner attitudes of their minds, can change the outer aspects of their lives." We may not be able to do much about our IQ which most believe is "fixed" at birth but we can do a great deal about our EQ (emotional intelligence). Some of the most encouraging lines from the *Quick Book* are:

> Great discovery! Your brain is like plastic. "Plasticity" is the term neurologists now use to describe the brain's ability to adjust to pressure and change.... A single cell can grow 15,000 connections with its neighbors.[1]

None of this tired old "this is just the way I am" or "you can't do much about genes" (which you can't). But we can do a great deal about the way we respond to the emotions that spring up within us.

First, we have to be aware of what is going on. To repeat this bit of wisdom from John Powell: "I have learned that when I become angry it is not helpful to ask the other person, 'Why did you make me so angry?' The wise response is to ask myself, 'What is in me that caused me to respond with such angry to what was said or done?'" Blaming the other for my emotional response assumes that someone else is responsible for the way I feel. It assumes that others cause me to feel and react the way I do. (No self-differentiated leader **ever** makes these assumptions.)

THE CHOICE IS OURS

"We have a choice in how we respond to emotions"[2] is the key to making progress in emotional intelligence. The four basic emotional intelligence skills are: self-awareness, self-management, social awareness, and relationship management. These lines are worth framing:

> Emotions always serve a purpose. Because they are reactions to your life experience, they always come from somewhere....Self-management is your ability to use your awareness of your emotions to stay flexible and direct your behavior

---

[1] Travis Bradberry and Jean Greaves, *The Emotional Intelligence Quick Book* (New York: Simon & Schuster, 2005), 81-82.
[2] Ibid, 10.

positively. This means managing your emotional reactions to situations and people.[1]

All of these ideas keep the all in my court and prevent me from ever adopting a victim attitude. It cannot be said too often: I am responsible for myself. I cannot shift that responsibility (or any part of it) to anyone else. I decide. I choose. Times and circumstances may make those decisions and choices very difficult but they remain mine.

Once I begin to take responsibility for my responses, everything changes. This has not been easy for me so why did I think it would be easy for the members of my congregations? I never heard any of my pastors talk about examining the thoughts behind the emotions we experience. (All emotions are derivatives of five core feelings: happiness, sadness, anger, fear, and shame. The range of intensity for each is quite wide. See chart on page 95 of *The Emotional Intelligence Quick Book*). Good questions are: What is behind this emotion I am experiencing? What is the thinking that has contributed to this kind of response? What influences in my past have come to play in this situation?

One of the challenges in intentional interims is leading people to acknowledge ownership of their emotions and perceptions. In discussions, it is refreshing to hear someone say: "This is why I think I have come to my position on this issue. There may be other contributing factors, but these are the ones I am able to identify." Keeping people speaking from the "I" position is the greatest challenge of all. Whenever anyone came to me with, "Many people are quite upset over your decision to…." I wanted to respond (but didn't) with, "You and who else?" Speaking from the "I" position is the quickest way I know to reduce anxiety and lower the level of conflict.

Knowing we have a choice and claiming responsibility for that choice changes the conversation. The decision to speak only for oneself means you don't have to spend any time postulating the motives behind what others say or do. My great rule of thumb: You

---

1 Ibid, 29.

only judge people by what they say or do; you do not pass judgment on what you believe prompted those words and actions. Many a conversation in my office with a disgruntled church member included: "I know what they really meant by that. You don't know them like I do." Of course, I immediately let the person know that we cannot have a discussion about someone else, we can only talk about the feelings of the person before me. Big rule in any healthy relationship: no triangles allowed!

My biggest decision (which I announce at the beginning of my interims) is that I base my responses on what is said to me and actions that are taken. I have no crystal motive-ball in which to gaze. And I take only first-person information, no second-hand data is permitted.

THE SOCIAL ANIMAL

> We are all embodied and enculturated, socialized into sets of values, economic structures, religious systems, political processes…Jesus lived in a concrete matrix of cultural, social, religious, and economic structures…. His restructuring of meaning was not a historical, and the ongoing work of the church remains embedded in evolving contexts.[1]

The author of the above quote summarizes this idea: "'Social location' is a code word for the insight that every person is born into a particular geographical place, financial circumstance, family configuration, ethnic subculture, set of social expectations…."[2] This remains true of those who gather on Sundays to worship together; they do not leave their social locations at home. After a sermon one Sunday morning, a seminary student confronted me with the question, "Is that a sermon you would preach to the homeless people on Market Street?" I believe I rightly perceived this (from tone of voice and facial expression) as a veiled attack on the rather affluent congregation I was serving. My response was simple and

---

1   Cynthia Crysdale, *Embracing Travail* (New York: Continuum, 2001), 58-59.
2   Ibid, 71.

calm (one of my better responses!) and the student did not make a further appearance.

What I wanted to tell her was that a large part of the minister's task is to address the people in their social location. How could a sermon for that congregation and a sermon for the homeless possibly be the same? There is biblical evidence for such a position. Each of Paul's letters is written to a specific congregation in a specific setting with specific problems. Although we have come to view his words as part of Holy Scripture, a key to solid interpretation begins with an awareness of the social location of the text. A little study reveals that the four Gospels were addressed to different audiences resulting in slightly different emphases. For example, Matthew writes to a Jewish audience and Jesus is plainly the new Moses. One example: compare Moses receiving the commandments on the mountain and Jesus' Sermon on the Mount.

We ignore social location at our peril. It is an obvious beginning place in ministry and in relationships. The only way to discover very much about social location is for people to tell you. Questions such as: "Tell me about your family. What are the things you remember about your childhood, your experiences in church? What are the most important things that you believe have shaped your life? Who are the people who have had the greatest impact on your life?" are only a few of the questions addressed to social location. Discovering social location takes time and listening skills that are often in short supply.

When we take time to tell each other our stories, the response is always the same: "I feel I know you so much better now." In one church, we had a series of Wednesday night sessions titled "My Pilgrimage of Faith." A number of persons told their stories; I began the series by telling my own story. These sessions were well attended and did **not** include a time for questions and feedback. We were not there to sit in judgment or to attempt to seek information the speaker had chosen not to give. We were there for the best thing we ever do for each other: non-judgmental listening. The amazing thing was the variety of social locations that surfaced in a congregation that appeared fairly homogeneous.

A book recently recommended to me was *The Social Animal* by David Brooks.[1] It is both interesting and eye-opening. Worthy quotes abound. I give you a few:

> The research being done today reminds us of the relative importance of emotion over pure reason, social connections over individual choices, character over IQ, emergent, organic systems over linear, mechanistic ones, and the idea that we have multiple selves over the idea that we have a single self.[2]

> Kenneth Dodge: "All information processing is emotional in that emotion is the energy that drives, organizes, amplifies, and attenuates cognitive activity and in turn is the experience and expression of this activity."[3]

> French babies cry differently than babies who have heard German in the womb because they've absorbed the French lilt of their mother's voice.[4]

> The next clear finding from research is that people are pretty bad at judging what will make them happy. People vastly overvalue work, money, and real estate. They vastly undervalue intimate bonds and the importance of arduous challenges.[5]

Rebecca Price Janney argues quite convincingly that the secular mass media has supplanted the church as "the keeper of the keys to the American way of life."[6] To my way of thinking, this calls not so much for protest as for recognition. Lamenting and lambasting the culture in which we live are exercises in futility. This is the culture in which we are called to live, minister, and witness. Our great national rallying days have to do with such events as the Super

---

1 David Brooks, *The Social Animal* (New York: Random House, 2011).
2 Ibid, xiii.
3 Ibid, 22.
4 Ibid, 11.
5 Ibid, 196.
6 Rebecca Price Janney, *Who Goes There?* (Chicago: Moody Publishers, 2009), 145f.

Bowl, March Madness, and (if you live in Louisville) the Kentucky Derby Festival. We are not going to change that in the one or two hours each week we have the opportunity to speak about the culture of the Kingdom. Again, awareness is the key.

SEEING THINGS IN A NEW WAY

"I can think only in pictures," the physicist and chemist Peter Debye declared. "It's all visual." We are told that is the way we all think. I vividly remember as a young person hearing my pastor preach and inserting in the sermon one of his most famous lines, "Did you get that or do you want me to draw you a picture?" This time an eager and enthusiastic youngster near the front, called out, "Draw us a picture, Brother ......!" After the laughter subsided, the pastor responded, "Maybe next time." He never again used that question, even though it remains true that we need to "see" what is being said.

Jesus' first word in his public ministry was "repent" (Mark 1:15). That word is the translation of a Greek word that means first of all "a change of mind." (It has little to do with being filled with sorrow and regret.) It means a new way of coming at life, a new way of seeing things, a new attitude about life. Jesus' parables were intended to provoke a change in perspective. They were meant to draw verbal pictures that brought the response, "I never saw it like that before." The story we call the parable of the prodigal son ends with the picture of the wayward son inside the father's house at a party and the father standing outside the door imploring the older son to come in and join the festivities. Jesus' story brings a picture of God that took his listeners by surprise. It was a new way to see in God's love the inclusiveness and the seeking for every person.

"If we change the way we see, we can change the way we respond."[1] If we can see ourselves as the prodigal, welcomed into the father's house, fully accepted, fully received, fully loved, it makes a difference in the way we live. When I stand before any congregation on a Sunday morning, I try to remember that many of the people

---

1   Elizabeth Lesser, *The New American Spirituality* (New York: Random House, 1999), 123.

before me do not feel that unconditional acceptance and love and that many of their responses reflect that perception. So much fear and anger on the part of church members stems from an inability to confess with Thomas Merton: "Who am I? I am one loved by Christ."[1]

Jesus' central message was one of God's mercy and love and the challenge to open one's life to receive these gifts of grace. One of the saddest questions in the Bible comes from Esau who pleads with his father Isaac, "*Oh, haven't you saved even one blessing for me?*" (Genesis 27:36, NLT). To feel you are the unblessed child leaves a deep scar that most find difficult (or impossible) to overcome. I have often wondered, "How many of the people in my congregations really feel unblessed?" I suspect the number is right up there with those who feel unloved. My attempt continues to help people with whom I minister to "see" the pictures these Scriptures bring:

> *...the Lord is thinking about me right now.* (Psalm 40:17, NLT)

> *Give thanks to the Lord, for his steadfast love endures forever.* (II Chronicles 20:21)

> *Your plans for us are too numerous to list.* (Psalm 4:5, NLT)

> *The Lord will work out his plans for my life ...* (Psalm 138:8, NLT)

> *And may you have the power to understand, as all God's people should, how wide, how long, how high, and how deep his love really is.* (Ephesians 3:18, NLT)

> *We love because he first loved us.* (I John 4:19)

---

[1] James Finley, *Merton's Palace of Nowhere*, 96.

TRANSFORMATION BY THE RENEWAL OF THE MIND

> *Do not be conformed to this world, but be transformed by the renewal of you minds ...* (Romans 12:2a)

> *Don't copy the behavior and customs of this world, but let God transform you into a new person by changing the way you think.* (Romans 12:2, NLT)

The entire Sermon on the Mount provides a new way of looking at things. The call to "repent," to have a change of mind, is an ongoing process. It begins with the recognition of how and why I see things now as I do. Carrie Fisher once confessed, "I was street smart – unfortunately the street was Rodeo Drive." This recognition has to precede seeing things in a different way. An honest appraisal of how we see and why we come at things as we do involves ongoing self-revelations.

I can remember making nursing home rounds one day when I was tense and feeling perfectly miserable. The thought of listening to one more patient recite their litany of complaints was almost more than I could bear. But the next patient I saw didn't offer a single complaint. She was a lovely 92-year-old lady with a saintly disposition. To this day I'm convinced she read my mind.

"Sit down, dear," she said as I walked in the room. "You look like it's been a long day." I was disappointed that my appearance was so transparent. "It must be exhausting taking care of old people all day long. I bet you get tired of hearing their complaints."

I must have looked positively dumbfounded as she continued. "I get tired of hearing the other residents here complain but I know they're just lonely and looking for a little sympathy." By this time I thought I saw a halo forming over her head. "Don't you let them drain you though, dear.. You get some rest and have a life of your own while you're still young. You deserve to be happy."

I'm sure that wonderful woman had no idea how much her selfless words touched me.[1]

My interpretation of what occurred is that this elderly woman had a different way of seeing the other residents (granted, it was easier for her) and she helped the counselor acknowledge her feelings and provided an insight into a different way of seeing things. I use this illustration because I think pastors need such people around on occasion to get us back on track. Proverbs 4:23 cautions: "Above all else, guard your heart, for it affects everything you do.". Heart refers to our understanding, our attitudes, our beliefs, our thoughts. Our healthy relation building beliefs and attitudes do not remain fixed. They need constant care and, sometimes, regeneration. They need to be carefully guarded because they really do affect everything we do.

QUESTIONS FOR REFLECTION AND DISCUSSION

1. How much time does your congregation spend in listening to one another's stories (the contexts from which members come)?

2. In what ways have you changed your EQ? What are you now working on?

3. How difficult is it to acknowledge ownership of our emotions and perspectives? Why is this?

4. How important is social location in determining approaches, ministry, and mission for a congregation?

5. What has brought about the changes in the way you look at things?

---

1 Mary O'Brien, *Successful Aging* (Concord, CAalifornia: Biomed General, 2005), 104-105.

Forget about Perfection

THE BIBLICAL WITNESS

If you wait for perfect conditions, you will never get anything done. (Ecclesiastes 11:4, NLT)

The disagreement (between Paul and Barnabas) became so sharp that they parted company … (Acts 15:39a)

I fear that when I come, I may find you not as I wish, and that you may find me not as you wish; I fear that there may perhaps be quarreling, jealousy, anger, selfishness, slander, gossip, conceit, and disorder. (2 Corinthians 12:20)

You must make allowances for each other's faults and forgive the person who offends you. (Colossians 3:13a, NLT)

CONTEMPORARY WISDOM

"God can carve the rotten wood and ride the lame horse."[1]

The Jewish Bible has not a single perfect person….So if these people were so flawed, why do we still read about them?…

---

1 Attributed to Martin Luther.

Simple. These men and women were great because they struggled to do right amid a predilection to do otherwise.[1]

Once you stop fearing failure, you're free.[2]

Whenever we can appreciate the goodness and value of something, while still knowing its limitations and failures, this also marks the beginning of wisdom and nondual consciousness. Most humans are not very good at such "allowing."[3]

R. E. C. Bowne, in his chapter on the essential untidiness of preaching, says, "The tidy mind is not the truthful mind; the utterance that leaves no room for doubt or place for question is the fruit of a mind that is full of unwarranted conclusions." The task of the faithful preacher, then, is deliberately to preserve an "untidy mind" so as to maintain an internal honesty about the ambiguities of daily life as it is actually experienced, both by him and by those to whom he preaches.[4]

PERFECTION IS NOWHERE TO BE FOUND

Jonathan Edwards' goal was to purge the church of all who strayed from the Puritan cultural code. He resolved to measure every parishioner's saintliness by his or her conformity to Christ's law. New applicants for church membership were judged by an even stricter standard. For four years not a single applicant was able to pass Edwards' strict tests of moral obedience.... Members of the Northampton church finally removed him from their church.[5]

All such efforts to maintain the purity of a church have met with similar results. John Calvin's Geneva was a place I don't think any of us would have wanted to live and yet I have never doubted

---

1   Shmuley Boteach, *Renewal* (New York: Basic Books, 2010), 69.
2   Fred Epstein, *If I Get To Five* (New York: Henry Holt, 2003), 77.
3   Richard Rohr, *The Naked Now*, 106.
4   Thomas R. Swears, *Preaching To Head and Heart* (Nashville: Abingdon Press, 2000), 75.
5   Robert C. Fuller, *Religious Revolutionaries* (New York: Palgrave Macmillan, 2004), 33.

his sincerity in wanting to establish a true "city of God." Jonathan Edwards was doomed to continuing frustration in his attempts to pastor the perfect church. (I have often wondered how he believed he was able to pass his own strict tests.)

These Reformation giants for whom the Bible was their source of authority evidently ignored some very clear messages. David and Diana Garland wrote a book titled *Flawed Families of the Bible* which challenges the assumption that it is filled with "family values." "The stories of families in the Bible are raw and uncensored"[1] is a good summary statement of their excellent book. The raw and uncensored is ameliorated by pieces of insightful humor:

> As one woman has said, "The only thing normal in our family is the knob that says Normal on the clothes dryer."[2]

> Sometimes, all God helps us do is to survive.[3]

> From Anne Lamott: "Everything is going to be Okay but we do not know exactly what Okay might look like."[4]

In the "Contemporary Wisdom" section we cited Shmuley Boteach's observation that "the Jewish Bible has not a single perfect person." The great question is not why our churches are not perfect, but where we ever got the idea that they could be! This is the greatest unrealistic expectation of them all! The old saw is still true: If I were to find the perfect church, I couldn't join it because, if I did, it would no longer be perfect. When I hear the charge that "the church is full of hypocrites," I ask for a definition of hypocrite. Biblically, it had to do with being a play actor, wearing a mask that hid the true person underneath. It had to do with pretending to be something you were not – like, pretending to be perfect! Most who bring the hypocrite charge believe church members are not

---

1 David and Diana Garland, *Flawed Families of the Bible* (Grand Rapids: Brazos Press, 2007), 13.
2 Ibid, 15.
3 Ibid, 33.
4 Ibid, 35.

living up to all they are supposed to be – and that is true. We have not left the sinner category (those who fall short of the glory God intends for our lives) just because we are members of the church.

Matthew Kelly speaks for me when he writes: "I have not had much experience with being perfect, but I have had considerable experience with making progress."[1] That statement comes following his dictum: "Practice doesn't make perfect. Practice makes progress."[2] That is all we can hope for. That is what Christian discipleship is all about. In another place I quoted a prayer I remember hearing that went something like this: "I'm not all I should be. I'm not all I can be. I'm not all I'm going to be. But, thank God, I'm not all I used to be!"

AS IT WAS IN THE BEGINNING

I have always treasured a remark attributed to Horace Greeley when someone lamented, "Your newspaper is not as good as it used to be." His reply, "It never was." The New Testament church was never all it was intended to be. If Paul couldn't get the perfect church organized what makes me think I could an ever do it? The phrase "as it was in the beginning, so it is now, and so it shall ever be" is the recognition that imperfection is built into the fabric of all human relationships: family, community, nation, and church. We can't reach perfection but we can make progress.

"Let's get back to the New Testament church" is a cry I have heard countless times during my years of ministry. In later years, my response was, "Oh, I hope it's not the church at Corinth!" The assumption is that in its early days the church was everything it was intended to be; we have now slipped from that ideal state and a new reformation is long overdue.

There are enough New Testament passages to indicate that the church continues to be what it has always been – a collection of "saints" who usually find it difficult to live up to their calling. "Saints" is Paul's favorite term for members of the body of Christ. 1 Corinthians 1:2 literally reads: "*called out saints.*" The word *saint*

---

[1] Matthew Kelly, *Perfectly Yourself* (New York: Ballantine Books, 2006), 21.
[2] Ibid, 12.

indicates a designation, not a superior moral or ethical achievement. God's gathered saints retain their full humanity.

The disagreement between Paul and Barnabas over Mark's participation in their mission became so contentious that the two parted company. Barnabas took Mark and left for Cyprus and Paul chose Silas to accompany him on his journey. Conflict over "church staff" erupted in the early days of the church and between two whom we thought would never have such a sharp disagreement.

In writing to the troubled congregation at Corinth, Paul expresses his fear that when he makes a personal visit he will find *quarreling, jealousy, anger, selfishness, slander, gossip, conceit, and disorder* (2 Corinthians 12:20). Things seem to have gotten way off track. This is especially shocking when you recall that this is a church Paul founded. You may wonder why he didn't get it "right." When you are dealing with people there is no way to get it "right" – if you mean avoiding conflict and maintaining an atmosphere of harmony and good will.

If things were not bad enough with the eight above mentioned problems in the Corinthian congregation, the one that has always taken me aback is what seemed to be happening during the Lord's Supper. Dinner was hosted in a home where the Lord's Supper was a part of the gathering. Paul's charge is that some people were bringing disgrace to the church by getting drunk during the celebration (1 Corinthians 11:21.)

Even Paul's beloved church at Philippi, to whom he could write, "*Every time I think of you, I give thanks to my God*" (Philippians 1:3, NLT), was far from perfect. Notice how things shift as he nears the end of his letter:

> *Dear brothers and sisters, I love you and long to see you, for you are my joy and the reward for my work. So please stay true to the Lord, my dear friends. And now, I want to plead with those two women, Euodia and Syntyche. Please, because you belong to the Lord, settle your disagreement.* (4:1-2, NLT)

We have no information about the nature of their quarrel but it was serious enough that Paul felt compelled to call their names and urge them to patch up things. (Most believe they were persons in prominent leadership positions.) Flawed humanity often triumphed in the church that was probably Paul's favorite and the one of which he was most proud.

MAKING PEOPLE FEEL NORMAL

It doesn't take long in an interim for people to begin to tell me in a whisper: "We are a divided congregation." "We've got lots of problems." "I think our last pastor simply gave up on us." "In spite of our conflict, we have a lot of good people in this church." "We are really not a bad group of people."

One of my primary tasks in a troubled congregation is to help the people feel "normal." To help them see they are not too different from people in any other church. Sometimes one of our workshop exercises will be the assignment to find passages in the New Testament that mention church "problems." When reporting out, many confess their surprise at what they found and gratitude that their church doesn't have all of those problems!

One church member told me, "We're not bad people; we've just got some bad problems." He went on to say that he didn't believe the serious unresolved issues defined the congregation; they were not their problems. We often find ourselves defining someone by their problems. "She is an alcoholic," is not a fair description. She is a person who is an alcoholic. "He is an old man," is another misnomer. He is a man who happens to be old. The identity and value of persons as human beings created in the image of God may be distorted but it does not erase that identity. Church congregations may get embroiled in conflict but that does not mean they have ceased to be church.

Colossians 3:13 in the NRSV reads: *Bear with one another, and, if anyone has a complaint against another, forgive each other, just as the Lord has forgiven you, so you must forgive.* The NLT reads: *You must make allowances for each other's faults and forgive the person who offends you. Remember, the Lord forgave you, so you must forgive others.* Complaints, faults, and offenses are all part of living together. That is why forgiveness is an ongoing requirement for

In Changing Times

healthy ongoing relationships. To make allowance for each other's faults is the acknowledgment of reality. We all have faults and we do not leave them at home when we come to church. That is the normal situation.

In helping normalize things, I have used this idea: "Maybe God's Hall of Fame is like baseball's, filled with superstars who got on base only once in every three attempts."[1] Once again, the focus is not on strike-outs, but on times of achievement.

SEEKING TO AVOID CONFLICT USUALLY RESULTS IN GREATER CONFLICT

In contrast to those who give the kind of comments mentioned in the previous section, at the beginning of an interim pastorate I am often told, "We really don't have any problems." A few months later, some of these same persons will take me aside to confess, "I didn't realize some people feel the way they do about how things are going in our church." The purpose of what I do is not to seek to unearth as many problems as possible but to create a safe atmosphere in which people feel free to discuss matters of concern.

In a workshop activity, I ask the participants to try to remember a time when a conflict in their church was addressed and managed with a positive outcome. I ask them to tell me how they believe this happened. I also ask, in the same workshop, for them to recall issues that could have been disruptive but were handled without major conflict. My question: How did this happen? If it is not already evident, it will become apparent in the way I conduct such workshops; we major on past achievements, strengths, and positive results. I never ask a congregation, "Tell me about your problems."

If I were to tell you that when the warning light on my auto dashboard came on with the message "check engine oil," I solved the problem by placing a sticker over the red light so I wouldn't see it, you would shake your head in disbelief. Yet, rarely do ministers or churches take action at the first warning sign of brewing conflict.

---

1 Philip Goldberg, *Road Signs on the Spiritual Path* (Boulder: Sentient Publications, 2006), 152.

They usually wait until it escalates (as it usually does) to the point where management is much more difficult and sometimes impossible. The best rule of thumb for cars and congregations: Don't ignore the warning lights. Address the issues at the first indications of needed maintenance.

Most ministers want to avoid conflict and I count myself among their number. When conflict rears its ugly head, we look for workshops on "Conflict Resolution" but all we can find are workshops on "Conflict Management." The second is within the realm of possibility, the first is not.

One of the most helpful books I have found in helping congregations to understand the nature of conflict is Speed Leas' *Moving Your Church Through Conflict*. (It is available only as a download through The Alban Institute but might also be found as a used book.) Leas identifies these levels of conflict:

- A. Level One: Problem to Solve
- B. Level Two: Disagreement
- C. Level Three: Contest
- D. Level Four: Fight/Flight
- E. Level Five: Intractable Situations
- F. Level Zero: Depression

For each of these levels, Leas discusses the issue, emotions, orientations, information, language, objective, and outcome. This information is on a single page and is one of the most helpful things I have ever used with a congregation as we talked about conflict. The goal in conflict management is to keep differences of opinion at Level One, A Problem Toto Solve. In Leas' words: "…the goal is to push Levels 5 through 2 down to Level 1, and push Level 0 up to Level 1. By doing this, everyone can see and agree that 'we have a problem to solve."

TRY TO LIGHTEN THINGS UP

At the stage in which conflict can be managed, I have always tried reduce the levels of tension and anxiety with a little lightness of spirit. One of my book recommendations is *A Time to Laugh:*

In Changing Times

The Religion of Humor by Donald Capps.[1] His chapters include discussions of humor as saving psychic resources, stimulus to identity creation, soul maintenance, and the gentle art of reframing (one of the most helpful chapters for me. Capps has another book simply titled *Reframing*, published in 1990). One value of the book is the possible lightening up of things for the minister or church leader. If you are the least bit creative, you can find ways to use some of his pieces such as these two (the second is an abbreviated version):

> Three men and an Irish setter were sitting at a table playing poker. The stakes were high and an onlooker was amazed to see the dog win two hands in a row. "That's incredible," said the onlooker. "I've never seen such a smart dog." "He ain't all that smart," whispered one of the players. "Whenever he gets a good hand, he wags his tail."[2]

> Bob received a parrot for his birthday. The parrot was fully grown, with a bad attitude and a worse vocabulary. Every other word was an expletive. Bob tried everything he could think of (his many attempts are listed) but to no avail. Finally, in utter frustration he put the parrot in the freezer. The parrot squawked for a few moments and then was quiet. Bob feared the worst but opened the freezer and the parrot calmly stepped out onto his extended arm and said, "I'm sorry that I might have offended you with my language and my actions and ask for your forgiveness. I will endeavor to correct my behavior." Bob was astonished at the bird's change in attitude and was about to ask what had prompted such a dramatic change when the parrot said, "Sir, may I ask what the chicken did?"[3]

Laughter can change the atmosphere in which discussions are being held and can often assist us in seeing how truly funny we all are. I have mentioned earlier my use of humor in my work

---

1 Donald Capps, *A Time to Laugh: The Religion of Humor* (New York: Continuum Publishing, 2005).
2 Ibid, 54.
3 Ibid, 53.

with congregations. It is never used to sidestep or ignore the issues under discussion. My intention is to lighten things up a little bit and create a better context for serious deliberation.

THREE THINGS THAT NEED TO GO

"There are only three things you need to let go of: judging, controlling, and being right. Release these three and you will have the whole mind and twinkly heart of a child." Hugh Prather's advice works well for reducing the anxiety during conflict. In one workshop exercise, I supply this quote and ask those present to discuss at their tables how they think letting go of these three things might contribute to more productive relationships in all of life (family and church).

If judging, controlling, and being right can be exorcised (or at least significantly diminished) the level of conflict can be lowered to a more manageable level. Many have said that the real problem is not the conflict but the way we handle it. My highest compliment at the end of an interim was, "I still can't believe it. We were able to talk about things that earlier would have caused a church split." Of course, I didn't make this happen, they did.

The three things that need to go (judging, controlling, and being right), need to go first of all in the life and work of the pastor. Looking back on early ministries, I cannot believe the number of times I made full and ineffective use of all of these. It is difficult to be pastoral while in any of these modes. In my later years, I adopted Paul's thesis in his letter to the church at Rome:

> *For I long to visit you so that I can share a spiritual blessing with you that will help you grow strong in the your faith, but I also want to be encouraged by yours. In this way, each of us will be a blessing to the other.* (Romans 1:11-12, NLT)

When people know you are not judging them, not attempting to control them, and you do not have to always believe you are in the right, blessings begin to flow both ways and conflict usually remains at a manageable level.

QUESTIONS FOR REFLECTION AND DISCUSSION

1. What are the advantages of the progress over perfection approach?

2. How does the New Testament describe the churches in its pages?

3. How is avoiding conflict detrimental to the health of a congregation?

4. What do you see as the differences between conflict resolution and conflict management?

5. How can humor help us reframe a serious situation?

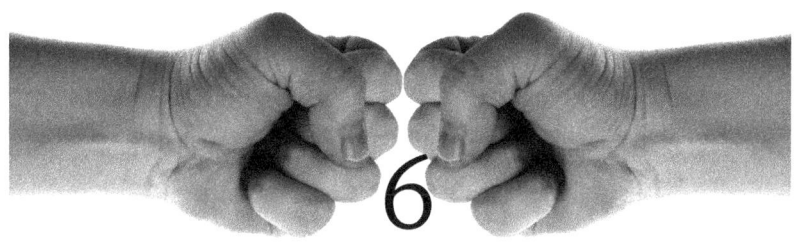

THE DANGERS IN LISTENING FOR THE APPLAUSE

THE BIBLICAL WITNESS

> *They do all their deeds to be seen by others.* (Matthew 23:5)

> *And if you don't brag about the good you do, then you will be truly wise!* (James 3:13, NLT)

> *For by the grace given to me I say to everyone among you not to think of yourselves more highly than you ought to think, but to think with sober judgment, each according to the measure of faith that God has assigned.* (Romans 12:3)

> *John said to him, "Teacher, we saw someone casting out demons in your name, and we tried to stop him, because he was not following us."* (Mark 9:38)

CONTEMPORARY WISDOM

> "I learned from my father that if you're just looking to take bows, you'll always be disappointed because the applause is never loud enough."[1]

---

1 Alan Alda, *Things I Overheard While Talking to Myself*, 83.

> The essence of their (Pharisee's) comfort zone was being applauded, being complimented, being respected, and being openly referred to. They further found significance when they compared themselves with others – always people they could safely label "sinners."[1]

> How do you persuade a Pharisee to give to the poor? Hire a couple of trumpeters. How do you get a Pharisee to pray? Give them an audience. How do you get a Pharisee to fast? Allow him to let it show.... They were starving for recognition.... The problem with Pharisees was they so often had no objectivity about themselves.[2]

WHAT WILL THE NEIGHBORS THINK?

I once thought the origin of this "mantra" might be biblical. It is not. As a child it conveyed the message: the neighbors are always watching and it is important to know what they think. It has taken me almost a lifetime to come to my corrective on that thesis: most "neighbors" are not looking at us and what they "think" is not the standard by which I am to live my life.

> I have a non-Christian friend who says he can spot Christians at Hollywood parties: "They worship at the altar of other people's approval."[3]

This is the quickest altar to find and the most seductive. It shifts the focus to others and permits them to determine how we are doing. What they think becomes what we ought to think. I did a sermon based on Matthew 23:5 I called "Who's Holding the Cue Cards?" Early television "live" programs provided instruction cards for the audience as well as the performers. The "applause" card

---

1 R. T. Kendall and David Rosen, *The Christian and the Pharisee* (New York: Faith Words, 2006), 153.
2 Ibid, 157-159.
3 Paul CouglinCoughlin, *No More Christian Nice Guy* (Minneapolis: Bethany House, 2005), 45.

In Changing Times

cued the audience to respond in a prescribed way. (There were no "laugh now" cards; augmented "canned laughter" was used when necessary. Without a live audience, it became the only laughter.) The cue cards were the performers' stock in trade.

Similar questions are, "Who's providing me with the signals that are determining the way I'm playing the game?" "To whom am I listening for the cheers of approval?" "Who are the persons that have taken the place of those 'neighbors' about whom I seemed to be so concerned?" A good exercise is to ask workshop participants to complete the statements: "In making decisions, I usually consider what _____ will think about what I have done. The reason I do this is _____." This is not as simple as it sounds. Sometimes those whose opinions matter to us may no longer even be around!

Another way of coming at this issue is to ask: "How do we evaluate what we are doing? On what basis do we measure the effectiveness of our ministries and programs? Who/what determines for us how well we are doing?"

Sidebar: A suggested activity: Answer honestly: "Is there anything I really want to do that I have never done because I am afraid of what others might think? What would I begin to do immediately if I didn't care what others might think?"

CHOOSING APPROVAL OVER AUTHENTICITY

In choosing approval rather than authenticity – our center of gravity is in "them" and not in ourselves. And what has been lost? Just the one true and vital part of us: our own yes-feeling, which is our capacity for growth.[1]

This is the classic "Are we other-directed or inner-directed?" question. (This does not rule out evaluation, which we will discuss later.) Jesus' primary criticism of the Pharisees was that they were not authentic. That is why he labeled them "hypocrites" or play-actors. You could never know who they really were because they were always acting out a role, playing the part they perceived would bring the greatest recognition. As a result, they didn't know who they were.

---

1 Gregg Levoy, *Callings* (New York: Three Rivers Press, 1997), 195.

Susan Sparks in *Laugh Your Way to Grace* has this quote from John Kenny: "If you don't know who you are, you act like you ain't."[1] You may need to think about this a moment before you "get it." If we don't know who we are, we live out our lives being someone else! Being authentic, having integrity, comes before all else. This applies to both pastor and parishioners.

Kirk Douglas tells of his lifelong resolve to pick up hitchhikers whenever it was feasible. One afternoon he picked up a sailor on leave. After jumping into the car and throwing his backpack into the back seat, the sailor did a double take, then a triple take, and then blurted out to Douglas, "Hey, man, do you know who you are?"[2]

Whenever I have been asked, "Don't you believe you could do ministry in one place just as well as another?" my answer is, "No." I have always felt that being in the right place at the right time is the key. This means I believe in a specific call to a specific place. When the "fit" is right, I know I have begun ministry with the key ingredient taken care of. My gifts, strengths, and weaknesses mean that many situations are not viable options. The bottom line: I have to go where I believe I can be my best authentic self and major on doing what I believe I have been called to do and am capable of doing. This doesn't solve all the problems but it does eliminate a great many.

I have always questioned my wisdom in accepting one particular call. In the early weeks of my pastorate, a short drive out of the city led me past a large billboard with the greeting "Welcome to Klan Country." The church was fairly large with a great number of some of the best people I have ever known. However, there were a large number of people who were extremely to the "right" of everything. They had trouble with me from the beginning; I understand why. When I left after a few years, one of them told a member of another congregation, "We've been trying to get rid of him ever

---

1 Susan Sparks, *Laugh Your Way to Grace* (Woodstock: Skylight Paths Publishing, 2010), 14.
2 Leonard Sweet, *Postmodern Pilgrims* (Nashville: Broadman & Holman, 2000), 1.

since he arrived." Why? They wanted me to be something I was not and never could be without giving up my deepest convictions. Did I make a mistake in going there? Probably not, because it was one of the pastorates where I learned some of my greatest lessons.

My first rule: if you have to give up who you are, if you have to leave your integrity parked at the door, you are paying too high a price for being there. I wish I had read this statement years before I found it: "Don't be too quick to please those who don't like you. You may ruin the real you. Self-acceptance usually beats reformation as a change strategy anyway."[1]

BE HONEST IN YOUR ESTIMATE OF YOURSELVES

The above line is the New Living Translation of Romans 12:3. For pastors and for churches, some good questions are: "What are my gifts? What do I do best? What do I most enjoy doing? What are my strengths? What are my weaknesses? What am I not good at?" Contrary to what I once heard, our major project is not to shore up our weaknesses, to work on what we're not good at, but to become better and more proficient at what we do best. In other words, we major on our strengths.

In churches, this is often called "asset-based planning." One always included activity in an interim is asking, "What does your church do best? What are the gifts that are evident in your membership? What things in the past have brought the most satisfaction and produced the best results?" To ask, "Tell me where your church is the weakest. What are the things you think are dragging you down?" places the focus on the very areas where the church will probably never be strong because this would be placing the emphasis on things the church does not possess.

As pastor, I have always felt it to be much better to get help from others who were gifted at doing what I could not do very well. Most "job descriptions" are really "mission impossible" descriptions. I cannot do all things well and I have never met anyone else who could. The unrealistic expectations usually begin with the initial covenant between pastor and people. I just finished reading

---

1 John Cowan, *The Common Table* (New York: HarperBusiness, 1993), 36.

one that brought the inner response: "Not even Moses or Paul would qualify for this position. Where did they ever get the idea that **one** person could do all this?" The place to begin the reality checks are upfront with the search committee. If you accept a position with requirements you know you can't fulfill, conflict will come knocking on your door before you get unpacked.

Both pastor and church need to honestly say, "Here are things we think need to be done, but we are not gifted to do them. Are they really necessary? If they are, how can we find someone to lead us in their accomplishment? Or, is there another way to achieve what we are after?" These are the issues that must continually be raised in on-going evaluation.

EVALUATION TO KEEP US ON TRACK

Regular, frequent, agreed upon evaluation is probably the most neglected tension-reducing and conflict-reducing tool. The often touted "once a year" evaluation is not sufficient. During the passage of this much time, a needed simple course correction can become an impossible transition. Every pastor and every staff member needs a trusted small group with whom they meet at least every three months to "touch base." Asking, "How do you think things are going? What do you think are the best things I am doing? Have you heard things of which you think I ought to be aware? In my ministry, is there anything causing you concern? Are there any changes you believe I should make?"

The responses to such questions call for discussion and negotiation. The sooner we are aware of things that are "brewing" the better we can address issues we can keep from becoming reasons for dismissal. In a recent workshop, the speaker lamented that "one-third of clergy will be subject to forced termination." The subject of the workshop was "Improving Ministry Leadership Through Emotional Intelligence." The clergy who lose their jobs usually do not possess good emotional and relationship skills. They are slow to pick up on the non-verbal messages they receive from the congregation. Most of us do not pay close attention to emotional

In Changing Times

clues. The presenter in this workshop reminded us that emotions contain data we can learn to read better.

When I took the Emotional Intelligence Appraisal mentioned earlier, my overall score was 75. This was true of both my personal competence and my social competence. (I decided that if I didn't give honest answers to the questions the results wouldn't tell me anything about myself.) The good news was that my overall score of 75 is higher than 47% of all people in the world! Because I hope you will buy the book and take the test I give you the brief paragraph on my report that provides meaning for those with a score of 70-79. It appears under the heading "With a Little Improvement, This Could Be A Strength."

> You are aware of some of the behaviors for which you received this score and you are doing well with them. Other emotionally intelligent behaviors in this group are holding you back. Lots of people start here and see a big improvement in their emotional intelligence once it's brought to their attention. Use this opportunity to discover the difference and improve in the areas where you don't do as well.

This is one time I do need to give attention to places in my perception that are weak. Both the book and the report make suggestions about ways to improve the important awareness skills. The basic skill is paying better attention (better listening) to myself and to others. It is the call to be more aware of what is going on.

Unfortunately, I vividly remember when evaluation came too late. In one church, a minister of youth was recommended by the search committee without much input from me or the rest of the staff. We were told, "This is our recommendation. We would like for you to meet the person." We did and immediately some red flags went up. Because everyone on the committee had such strong positive feelings, we did not push our questions and concerns. Big mistake! Less than three months after the person began work, I began receiving alarming and specific complaints. Note: the search committee should have remained in touch with the youth minister and had **monthly** meetings for at least the first six months. Those who brought me their concerns were always asked, "Have you talked with the minister of youth about your concerns?" The most frequent response was, "Yes, and I couldn't get to first base." I always insist that anyone who has a concern about a staff member go to that individual and talk one-on-one. If the issue is not resolved then I agree to talk with the staff member. That is what I did next.

One of the most voiced concerns was the lack of Bible study for our youth. When I asked what was being done I was told, "I believe in living the Bible, not just studying it at the church." I asked how that was done and got this reply: "I take the youth to nursing homes and we walk through the hallways singing *Jesus Loves Me*." That was just the tip of the iceberg and the person was dismissed after six months with a great deal of fallout from search committee members and a few parents whose children had made a connection with the youth minister. It was one of the worst staff situations I ever experienced.

I once had a search committee member who threatened to resign if his choice was not selected. To "keep peace," the remainder of the committee acquiesced and the candidate proved to be a far from ideal choice. The person's gifts did not match the requirements for the position.

AGREED UPON CRITERIA

For effective evaluation, the criteria must be specific and the result of mutual agreement. "I never knew I was responsible for that," is indicative of information too late in coming. In one church where I was interim, it was the policy for the staff to present written reports at each monthly deacon's meeting. There was always time for questions and discussions. The staff members also met monthly with their respective committees and I had a monthly meeting with the deacon officers. I found this to be extremely helpful.

This process means that we are all providing cue cards and negotiating which ones will be permitted to provide the signals for our ministries. It means we are not comparing ourselves with others. Being better than or worse than has nothing to do with an agreed upon list of things that belong to us and for which we are responsible. Big sidebar: the church needs to be kept informed about agreed upon pastoral and staff responsibilities; the need may arise for discussion in a larger congregational setting. Too many discussions are held when it is too late for much course correction or redemption.

The expectations written and voiced at the beginning of one's ministry are subject to change without notice! That is why we need frequent intentional means to discover which ones are changing. In any relationship, expectations do not remain the same. We need the mechanisms in place so that we are alerted at the first indication of changing expectations. Pastors and churches need specific guidelines as to how pastor and people (staff and people) will remain in ongoing dialogue with one another. When you wait for a "called meeting" to learn what has been going on or to begin discussions on sensitive issues, adequate damage control becomes almost impossible.

EVEN IN THE BUSINESS WORLD

Good leadership has some basic elements regardless of where it is being exercised. Every pastor and church leader ought to be aware of the skills that enable people to function as healthy and productive leaders. Although the church is not a business (how many times have you heard that one?), we have much to learn from those who have demonstrated that they know how to enable people to work together for a common purpose (vision). What is commonly termed "people skills" is usually the major deficit in most conflicted congregations.

From Ken Blanchard's *The Heart of a Leader* I again draw three quotes worth discussing:

"Thanks for everything" is meaningless.[1]

Rick Tate: "Feedback is the breakfast of champions."[2]

---

[1] Ken Blanchard, *The Heart of A Leader*, 5.
[2] Ibid, 10.

> Servant leadership is more about character than style....I want to be led by strong natural servants because they are willing to use whatever leadership style – directive, supportive, or some combination – best serves the needs of those they lead.[1]

QUESTIONS FOR REFLECTION AND DISCUSSION

1. In what ways do we worship at the altar of people's approval? From whom (or what) do we take our cues?

2. In what ways do we choose approval over authenticity? Why do we make this choice?

3. What is your definition of humility?

4. Does your church have regular evaluation of all church staff? What tools are used and how has it worked?

5. How can evaluation be done in such a way as to not be interpreted as simply criticism?

---

1 Ibid, 128-129.

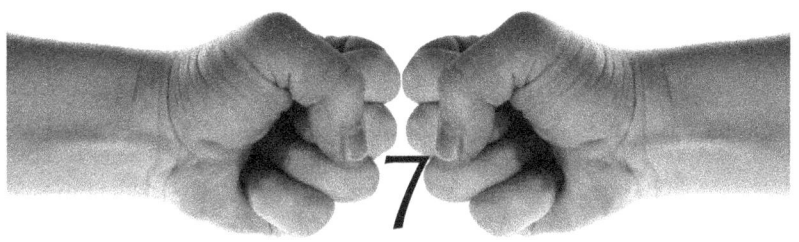

LIFE IS FULL OF ENDINGS

THE BIBLICAL WITNESS

> *For everything there is a season, and a time for every matter under heaven:*
> *a time to be born, and a time to die;*
> *a time to plant, and a time to pluck up what is planted;…*
> *a time to break down, and a time to build up;*
> *a time to weep, and a time to laugh;*
> *a time to mourn, and a time to dance;…*
> *a time to seek, and a time to lose;*
> *a time to keep, and a time to throw away….*
>
> (Ecclesiastes 3:1, 2, 3b, 4, 5a, 6)

> …[T]*his one thing I do: forgetting what lies behind and straining forward to what lies ahead, I press on toward the goal for the prize of the heavenly call of God in Christ Jesus.* (Philippians 3:13-14)

CONTEMPORARY WISDOM

> *I'll Never Get Out of this World Alive* song by Hank Williams

Resistance to change is a consistent reality in congregations.[1]

One day your life will flash before your eyes. Make sure it's worth watching.[2]

The past is not a fixed item. It's raw material waiting to be interpreted anew at each stage of your life. You need to make it talk in these interim periods, and as always, you need to listen to what it says.[3]

TOMORROW MAY NOT BE ANOTHER DAY

Perhaps the second most memorable line from the movie *Gone With The Wind* (the first is composed of Rhett Butler's final eight words in the film) is Scarlet O'Hara's, "I can't think about thatn now. If I think about that now, I'll go crazy. I'll think about that tomorrow. After all, tomorrow is another day." The Hank Williams song title above is the harsh reminder that tomorrow may not be another day. Life is full of endings, including the ending of life itself. We have only a limited amount of time; one day our time on earth will come to an end. Our pilgrimage will be over.

Rarely have I witnessed visible signs of shock on the faces of my congregation after I have made a particular point in a sermon. It happened on one occasion years ago and I don't think I would ever use the particular metaphor again. I was attempting to emphasize the importance of not postponing the things we know we ought to do and intend one day to do. That one day might never come. The comment that brought the wide-eyed shock was: "On this passage through life we are not on the Good Ship Lollypop; we are on the Titanic, and she's going down!"

The Bible is full of reminders that life is limited; none more graphically stated than in Psalm 90:9-10:

---

1 Richard Blackburn, *Leadership and Anxiety in the Church*.
2 Shumley Boteach, *Renewal*, 183.
3 Candice Carpenter, *Chapters* (New York: McGraw-Hill: 2002), 91.

> *For all our days pass away under your wrath; our years come to an end like a sigh. The days of our life are seventy years, or perhaps eighty, if we are strong; even then their span is only toil and trouble; they are soon gone, and we fly away.*

Verse 12 is the great "therefore" of this reality: So teach us to count our days that we may gain a wise heart. The New Living Translation is: " Teach us to make the most of our time, so that we may grow in wisdom." Knowing that one does not have forever, wisdom calls for making the most of the time we do have, for not living in a state of constant postponement, for knowing what time it is (Ecclesiastes).

Reminders of our mortality are reminders to use wisely the greatest gift we have – time. On the copyright page of *The Dilbert Principle*, the author's name appears with a missing item. It reads: Adams, Scott, 1957 - …. The final date is missing but one day it will be added. The most important part of that life-span indicator is the hyphen in the middle. We didn't have anything to do with the beginning date of our lives and we usually don't have very much to do with the second date. We have everything to do with the dash between the two. The challenge is obvious: we are called to live the dash!

The Last Lecture by Randy Pausch is a classic reminder and demonstration of that truth:

> Time is all you have. And you may find one day you have less than you think.[1]

When we asked (Dr. Wolff), "How long before I die?" he answered, "You probably have three to six months of good health." That reminded me of my time at Disney World. When you ask Disney World workers, "What time does the park close?" they're supposed to answer, "The park is open until 8 p.m."[2]

Randy Pausch used the time he had "open" to deliver his "last lecture" message to as many people as possible. In his lecture, he begins with the warning that those who are expecting a dark, neg-

---

1　Randy Pausch, *The Last Lecture*, 111.
2　Ibid, 63.

ative speech will be disappointed. If you have heard the lecture (available on DVD) you know it is filled with humor and its positive emphasis is captured in the title, "Achieving Your Childhood Dreams." His message to all of us is the same: regardless of our circumstances or any "diagnosis" we have received, we are still in the space between our two calendar dates, and the challenge is to invest fully in the time we have.

Often that investment involves the courage to face the ending of something in order to inaugurate the beginning of something.

ENDINGS COME BEFORE BEGINNINGS

Not only is there a final end of things, but along the way many things come to an end. Many who appear to have little difficulty accepting the fact of mortality seem to have great difficulty accepting the endings that are a part of our journey in time.

> The truth of the matter is, the only widely accepted lifestyle offered to our elders in this culture is to do everything they can to pretend they're still young![1]

Living on the basis of what is and not on the basis of what was is so logical that you wonder how we ever lost such basic wisdom. I keep posted a reminder given me by a delightful senior in one of my pastorates: "Senior Citizen: Doing the Best I Can with What I Have Left." Let me point out the obvious. I do not have everything left; that is acknowledged. But I do have a lot left and that will be my focus. I can no longer play tennis singles but that doesn't relegate me to the role of couch potato.

Accepting the changes that come in life means understanding that as one chapter concludes we have the opportunity to turn the page to a new chapter.

> The people in Maine are known for saying, "You can't get there from here," when asked for directions. In terms of life

---

1 John Welshons and Richard Carlson, *When Prayers Aren't Answered* (Novato CA: New World Library, 2007), 106.

directions, perhaps it is truer to say, "You can only get there if you are fully here."[1]

It is much easier to close out a chapter in life if that chapter has been relatively successfully lived. (Notice the important word "relatively!") I recently read that the number one problem experienced by most older adults is regret. Almost all of us look back and moan, "If I only could relive that chapter in my life I would certainly do things differently." (The most comforting word I ever found on that was from someone who suggested that if we had a portion of our lives to live over again we might do worse!)

Paul's example of *forgetting what lies behind* is his recognition that it must precede any attempt to strain *forward to what lies ahead*. If you refuse to close out a chapter, you will have great difficulty beginning a new one. You may find it is impossible. We all know people whose lives were put on hold because of a chapter they couldn't close. Great tragedies are often compounded because they become the barriers to moving ahead. We never "get over" the big hurts of life but there ought to come a time when we learn how to "get on" with life – even with our newly acquired scars.

We may never again "be the same" but we don't have to be in order to get on with life. After our grief, anger, fit pitching, and protests against the unfairness of just about everything, we can say, "Okay, now what's next?" Of course, this takes courage and faith and determination and persistence. I have heard a thousand times, "Old age is not for sissies." Life is not for sissies! My wife found a refrigerator magnet that had a prominent position for several high tension years. It read: "I'm going to quit. But not today." Those in AA gain sobriety one day at a time; it's only today that they have to keep their pledge. The time to turn the page on what is over and begin a new chapter is today. We'll just see what today holds as we write on page one of this new adventure.

---

1 Jon Kabat-Zinn, *Wherever You Go There You Are* (New York: Hyperion, 1994), 131.

NOT LESS, BUT MORE

Churches are notorious for refusing to shut down programs and ministries that have had their day. In one of my pastorates, we finally made the decision to discontinue the "regular" Sunday night service. A retired minister was a member of the congregation and he protested long and loudly. He let me know how disappointed he was that I had abandoned an important part of the church's tradition and one that he had made quite successful in every church where he had ministered. In his mind, it was still the fifties. Most churches in our area had much earlier discontinued this service and our attendance had become embarrassingly low. Training Union had been gone for years and, among other things, Sunday night had become a prime television night.

I, too, remembered as a boy the excellent Sunday night crowds and the place this important service had in the life of our church. You didn't have to plead with people to attend. The truth be told, there was not much else going on! It was another time in, literally, almost another world. It was time to cooperate with the inevitable. What we did in the church where the retired minister issued his complaint was to use Sunday nights for workshops, seminars, and special events that served our church far better than another "service as usual." We acknowledged an ending in order that there might be a new beginning.

Questions I always ask when serving as interim pastor: What programs no longer generate the enthusiasm and attendance they once did? Are there ministries and programs that are plainly no longer effective? What things are you simply weary of promoting? If you could eliminate any programs or ministries without fear of repercussions, what would they be? What do you no longer attend? In what do you no longer participate?

Taking the steps to close out that which is obviously no longer effective is one of the most difficult things churches ever do. "I remember the time when our Youth Choir was larger than the regular choir. Their annual tour was one of the biggest events of the year. We need to revive that choir and bring more our young people back." I heard that more times than I can count. The words of some of the youth musicals are still echoing in my head – and pleasantly so! I still remember the musical *Good News*. But that chapter is over. It may be possible in certain places and in modified forms but as a great sweeping youth movement, it is gone.

Although youth choirs are not completely gone, there is a greater emphasis now on youth mission projects and tours. The good news is that many young people are very enthusiastic about these opportunities. This is a new (and some feel better) chapter in youth ministries. When I ask questions about ending ineffective program and ministries I always add, "Are there any possibilities you see for something different to fill the void? Who would do this and how might it be done?" (Other questions always surface.) The emphasis is not on simply forgetting what used to be but committing to what lies ahead.

FREE TO GO AHEAD

An old farmer was in conversation with a university student who was doing a research paper on agricultural developments during recent decades. "I bet you've seen a lot of changes in your lifetime," commented the young man. "Yes, I have," responded the farmer, "and I've been against every one of them!" With the shaking of the foundations in just about everything in the world, many are resolved to maintain the church as their place of stability. Meaning: "As it was in the beginning, so it is now, and ever more shall be, world without end." Or to give the motto of too many churches: "Come weal or woe, our status is quo."

There is little we can do about the changing world around us. We are not responsible for much of what happens but we are responsible for how we respond to what happens. What is called for is not knee-jerk reaction but thoughtful response. A couple of quotes:

> A tailgater is just a tailgater until I make him my personal nemesis and seat a grievance beside me. Today take note of any personal conclusion you trip over and of every disposition you

stumble into. Today, hold to one simple idea: "I see what I decide and react as I choose."[1]

> The problem with the past is that it has no imagination; it can only repeat its script.[2]

It's okay to acknowledge our initial impulse with regard to a given situation. (Here is where emotional intelligence comes back in.) It is almost always unwise to go with that immediate gut reaction. Simply saying, "Okay, this is the way I feel but what is a better way of responding to what has happened?" is to put one on the road to response instead of reaction.

Churches need not only inspiration but also imagination as they think about how to respond to the situation in which they find themselves.

> Complexity theory is thus suspicious of long-range planning. We think more by flexibility and adaptability to changing circumstances than by long-range plans. They are marked more by vision than by detailed strategies. How many churches have brilliant long-range plans gathering dust on shelves because of unforeseen circumstances?[3]

In one church where I was interim, I was given a long-range plan that someone had discovered stored away in one of the supply rooms. That's where most of them end up. Circumstances change and never have they changed more rapidly or dramatically than in today's world. Deciding what to do for the next three to six months is now what many churches are doing. The problem with most long-range plans is that by the time they are released they are already out of date. In the time it took to get the plan together circumstances call for a modification in the plan.

---

1 Hugh Prather, *The Little Book of Letting Go*, 192.
2 James Hollis, *Why Good People Do Bad Things* (New York: Gotham Books, 2007), 64-65.
3 Howard Snynder, *Decoding the Church* (Grand Rapids: Baker Books, 2002), 42.

Imagination, flexibility, and *adaptability* need to be three words kept in the forefront of all "planning." Anything "set in stone" means at some point in the future it will take dynamite to dislodge it. These kind of explosions always have earthshaking repercussions! I know by experience. In another book I gave the account of a pastorate in which it became necessary to demolish the old sanctuary. A new one had been in service for a number of years; the old one was attached to the educational building, but was no longer being used for any purpose. We were informed by our insurance agent that his company could no longer insure the educational building because the old sanctuary was a fire hazard. After much discussion, it was decided that we would hold a memorial service for the old sanctuary and allow members to share memories about services and events in that building. At the conclusion of the service, our oldest active member removed the first brick from the condemned building.

It didn't take dynamite to remove that brick and in the spirit of a new beginning we were able to do some remodeling and updating of the educational building and provide some much needed new parking space. Acknowledging and honoring the chapter that was ending with demolition and looking ahead to something new enabled us to deal with necessary change without conflict. Being free to go ahead means that you give just as much thought to how you will end something as you do as to how you will begin something new. The thoughtful consideration for an ending includes consideration for how people are going to feel about bringing something to a close. The emotional elements in such situations are usually the most crucial.

Clifford Kuhn in his *Fun Factor* gives what he calls "The Fun Commandments." His tenth commandment is "Celebrate everything." This includes celebrating endings as we did in the church mentioned above. He says, "Celebration is made up of two elements – gratitude and joy."[1] Both of these elements were included in our service of remembrance for the former sanctuary (we did not refer to it as the "old" sanctuary). We acknowledged the loss and

---

1 Clifford Kuhn, *The Fun Factor,* 29.

the grief that was share in thinking about what would be no more, but the key ingredient in the service was gratitude and joy for both the people and the events represented in that brick and mortar.

YOU OFTEN HAVE TO BE VERY CREATIVE

The call for repentance needs to be issued to many churches. The basic meaning of the biblical word is the call for a change of direction, a change of mind, a change in the way we see things. It is the challenge to look at things in a new way. This challenge almost always offers a new opportunity.

Josh Gordon tells of serving as a camp counselor in the summer of 1976. The camp consisted of 60 seven-year-olds. The group had just returned from a long hike and was ready for lunch. The junior counselor, in panic mode, rushed up to Josh and informed him that, running out of center slices, a third of the peanut butter and jelly sandwiches had been made from the end pieces from loaves of bread. The junior counselor could imagine the reaction of those who had to make do with the ends of things.

Josh held one of the undesirable sandwiches in his hand and noticed that from the side view the sandwich curved to a point like the front of a rocket ship. Holding an "end" sandwich high above his head, Josh announced in a loud, clear voice: "I have good news and bad news. The good news is that we have something completely new here at camp today, an aerodynamically sound peanut butter and jelly sandwich." He then "zoomed" the sandwich through the air. Then he announced that there were only twenty of them. There was a stampede to grab those twenty sandwiches.

One seven-year-old's perception of the sandwiches after Josh Gordon's demonstration was: "Sandwiches made from two ends offer much less wind resistance than ordinary, boring sandwiches. Cool!"

That story comes from Josh Gordon's book, *Presentations that Change Minds*.[1] I found its insights applicable to much of what I am doing as an intentional interim minister and church consultant.

---

1 Josh Gordon, *Presentations That Change Minds* (New York: McGraw-Hill, 2006), 142-144.

In Changing Times

Especially helpful is a series of charts in Appendix B. Some of those charts are:
   Strategies Used Most Often.

- Strategies Most Persuasive.
- Most Persuasive Strategies (ranked in 8 industries).
- Most Hostile Audiences.
- Ways to Begin a Presentation.
- Building Trust.
- Biggest Trust Builders.

His book could just as easily be titled *Presentations That Help People See Things In A New Way*.

QUESTIONS FOR REFLECTION AND DISCUSSION

1. How difficult has it been in your life to deal with endings? Which brought the greatest challenges?

2. In what ways does a good "closure" contribute to a good "beginning"?

3. Are there programs and ministries in your church that are no longer effective but the emotional attachments prevent their being abandoned?

4. What is the extent of long-range planning that churches today can realistically attempt? How do the words "imagination," "flexibility," and "adaptability" shape that planning

5. Have you ever had a peanut butter and jelly sandwich "opportunity" (Josh Gordon)? How did it go?

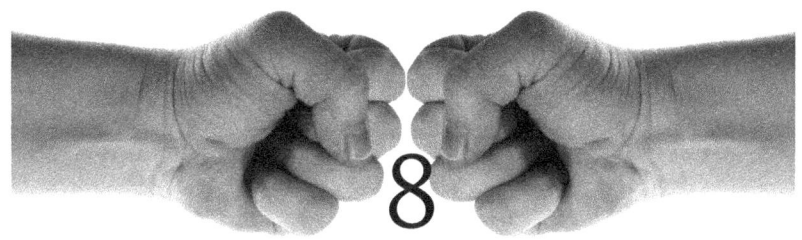

WE NEED EYES THAT SEE AND EARS THAT HEAR

THE BIBLICAL WITNESS

"Are your hearts hardened? Do you have eyes, and fail to see? Do you have ears, and fail to hear?" (Mark 8:17b-18a)

He said, "Go out and stand on the mountain before the Lord, for the Lord is about to pass by." Now there was a great wind…but the Lord was not in the wind; and after the wind an earthquake, but the Lord was not in the earthquake; and after the earthquake a fire, but the Lord was not in the fire; and after the fire a sound of sheer silence. When Elijah heard it, he wrapped his face in his mantle and went out and stood at the entrance of the cave. (1 Kings 19:11-13a)

CONTEMPORARY WISDOM

God is not more in a church that he is anywhere else. But what makes church holy in a special way is that we ourselves are more present in it.[1]

Have you never thought of listening with complete attention to a person you're having a conversation with as an ascetic discipline …? Whatever reality calls us to do, however

---
1 Frederick Buechner, *Secrets in the Dark*, 75.

trivial, is matter for moral, spiritual, mental, emotional – total growth, when we conscientiously strive to do it well and with awareness.[1]

When things are running well, I spend 20 percent of my time on the people process. When I'm rebuilding an organization, it's 40 percent. I'm not talking about doing formal interviews or selecting staff; I mean really getting to know people.[2]

MY HEAD IS MADE UP

I grew up on radio. Not "talk radio" but radio that opened the window to a world of imagination. *The Life of Riley* with William Bendix was a favorite. I often saw myself in this "hero" who frequently echoed his conviction with the phrase "My head is made up," only later to discover he was wrong. In hearing some questions and listening to others some new stuff came into his head that changed his opinion.

When Jesus tells his disciples to *beware of the yeast of the Pharisees and the yeast of Herod* (Mark 8:15), they believe they are being chastised for forgetting to pack bread for their boat trip. He reminds them of the recent feedings of the four thousand and the five thousand, and concludes with, *"Do you not yet understand?"* (8:21). In between these two questions, Jesus asks two other questions: *"Are your hearts hardened? Do you have eyes, and fail to see? Do you have ears, and fail to hear?"* (8:17b-18a).

Jesus' disciples had their heads made up so they really couldn't see or hear. The Kingdom that was being inaugurated with Jesus was about more grace, abundance, and inclusion than they had ever imagined. The disciples' understanding of the way faith and life "worked" was due for an overhaul. Those needed changes would come only if they could shake loose some of their fixed viewpoints.

---

1 Monks of New Skete, *In the Spirit of Happiness*, 82.
2 Larry Bossidy & Ram Charan, *Execution* (New York: Crown Business, 2002), 26.

Activity for workshop: What have been the major changes in your ideas about faith, the church, and life in general? Were most of these sudden or over a period of time? What led to these changes? Discuss these with those at your table.

A good Bible study project is to read through the Gospels noting every question Jesus asks. Likewise, it is worth noting all the questions God asks in the Old Testament. The biblical narrative hardly gets underway until God poses the two basic questions: "Where are you?" (to Adam) and "Where is your brother?" (to Cain). The remainder of Scripture explores the answers to these two questions: "Where are you in relation to God?" and "Where are you in relation to others?"

When God finally gives Job an audience, it is not with answers to Job's questions. The paradox is clearly stated:

> *Then the Lord ANSWERED Job out of the whirlwind: … Gird up your loins like a man, and I WILL QUESTION YOU, and you shall declare to me."* (Job 38:1, 3)

In our personal lives and in the church we need someone around who continues to ask us good questions. We also need to be able to ask ourselves and our congregation different questions. The old saw is true: If we keep asking the same questions we will keep getting the same answers.

> I was raised on a "Jesus is the answer" form of the faith, which implied that Christianity is the definitive answer to every single one of life's problems. Imagine my surprise to hear Alan Jones of Grace Cathedral in San Francisco say that the "task of the Christian minister is to guard the great questions."[1]

One of the things I like best about an intentional interim is that its purpose is not to provide answers or solutions to problems. A major ingredient in my work is to keep asking pertinent questions in order to allow the congregation to form the answers and solutions that are best suited to them. Guarding the great questions and asking the good questions (or better questions) should be our

---
1 Spencer Burke and Barry Taylor, *A Heretic's Guide to Eternity*, 103.

priority. Providing answers makes them "my" answers that frequently need defending. The defensive is always high risk territory.

Reflect and Discuss: What are some of the best questions you have ever heard? What are some of the questions that have changed your way of thinking? What/who was the source of those questions?

Another good exercise is to choose a topic that needs discussion and then ask each table to select two or three persons to give their points of view. The Quaker rule is to be adopted and those at the table may only ask questions for further clarification; they may not comment. Following this exercise, I ask what was different about their discussions from the way they were usually experienced.

A NEEDED COMMITMENT

> ...[T]his second kind of seeking consists in a commitment to paying attention to whatever comes to us in the expectation that everything belonging to God and being full of the glory of God – the familiar prayers of the liturgy, a dream, the neighbor's dog, an article in the newspaper, an exchange in the grocery store with a stranger – can reveal to us what we need to know.[1]

Too many have the Elijah frame of mind. In his world, divine revelations came most frequently in dramatic manifestations: wind, earthquake, and fire. To be told that *the Lord was not in the wind... the earthquake...* or *the fire* was revolutionary. For God to be in *the sound of sheer silence* or *the sound of a gentle whisper* (NLT) was most instructive for a prophet who had just witnessed God's fireworks on Mount Carmel.

The quote from the Monks of New Skete in "Contemporary Wisdom" is a reminder that we will miss much of what God has to say to us if we are tuned in only to the spectacular or to the frequency on which we are certain he communicates. Anything and anyone can become the avenue for revelation. Dreams are accepted channels of such revelation in both Testaments. Do we even consider this a possibility? Cultivating the discipline of noticing (as

---
1   Roberta Bondi, *In Ordinary Time* (Nashville: Abingdon Press, 1996), 65.

In Changing Times 99

Moses must have done, indicated by the writer's comment: *When the Lord saw that he had turned aside to see....*) is not easy in a world of overwhelming distractions.

> The story is told of President Franklin Roosevelt, who often endured long receiving lines at the White House. He complained that no one really paid any attention to what he was saying. One day during a reception he decided to try an experiment. He murmured to each person who passed down the receiving line, "I murdered my grandmother this morning." The guests responded with phrases like, "Marvelous! Keep up the good work." "We are proud of you." "God bless you, sir." It was not until the end of the line, while greeting the ambassador of Bolivia, that his words were actually heard. Nonplussed, the ambassador leaned over and whispered, "I'm sure she had it coming.[1]

"Pay attention!" was the remembered watchword in almost every one of my elementary school classes. "Does not pay attention" was the teacher's frequent notation on the comment segment of my report card. Paying attention is basic to the educational experience. It is the commitment to be present where we are in order to be aware of what is going on around us. It is the commitment to focus on the persons who are with us. It is our determination to accept the discipline of discipleship in Jesus' command that we have eyes that see and ears that hear.

WHY AREN'T PEOPLE TALKING TO ONE ANOTHER?

Hardly a day goes by without some reference to the polarization in our culture. An election year (2012) appears to be making this worse than ever. It is almost impossible to find an example of dialogue or of genuine debate (in the tradition of the famous Lincoln/Douglas debates). Usually, the opponent is dehumanized and demonized and, therefore, could not possibly have anything to contribute to the subject. Some years ago, a Louisville pastor

---

[1] Terry Felber, *Am I Making Myself Clear?* (Nashville: Thomas Nelson, 2002), 54.

wrote a guest editorial for our newspaper and included the offer to dialogue with anyone about his position. He did not receive a single request. He did receive some anonymous phone calls. One person offered to "punch out his lights."[1]

Long ago, I gave up simple solutions that begin with "our problem is" and I began to understand the complexity and connectedness of people, circumstances, and events that "define" our problem. At least one contributing factor to our inability to dialogue is illustrated in a newspaper article of two days ago. The religion writer gives the context for a particular divisive issue. One minister is convinced he is inspired by the Holy Spirit to take a particular stand and then is quoted: "I know our God who is holy is pleased with this action."

I immediately turned to my research material for this book and found the lines: "No one of us can hear the whole of God's voice…. To listen well is to listen with the ears of others as well as our own."[2] It just so happens that I have a different take on the issue presented in the newspaper article. Does that mean that I am not inspired by the Holy Spirit and that God is not pleased with my position? No room has been left for dialogue; the minister has heard the whole of God's voice and he does not need to listen with the ears of others as well as his own.

The infamous line "If you have the truth what is there to dialogue about?" sets too much of the tone for our time. "Reasoned discourse" does not mean that we are called to abandon what we believe. It means we are willing to listen with full attention to those with opposing points of view. My listening includes the genuine desire to understand why and how others see things as they do. I will, of course, expect the same kind of listening in return. Will positions be radically altered? Probably not, but we will have a much better understanding of one another and will have "maintained fellowship across honest differences of opinion." The words in quotes speak to

---

1 Joseph Phelps, *More Light; Less Heat* (San Francisco: Jossey-Bass, 1999), ix.
2 Frederick Schmidt, *What God Wants For Your Life* (New York: HarperCollins, 2005), 184.

In Changing Times

the kind of freedom of conscience my particular tradition used to practice. It now appears to be in rather short supply.

TRUTH IN UNORTHODOX PLACES

> A friend had suggested that I was looking for truth in unorthodox places, but that, of course, is where God often puts it.[1]

A sentence like the one above makes many people nervous because they believe God never colors outside the lines of orthodoxy. They believe you have to be careful what books you read and what movies you see. I have often thought about those who first heard Jesus' parables and the difference between their recorded responses and ours. "John Dominic Crossan says that a parable is an earthquake opening up the ground at your feet."[2] Our familiarity with the parables has turned most of them into types of Aesop fables with nice little morals at the end. When the religious leaders of Jesus' day heard his parables, they shouted, "This man has got to go!" They weren't about to look for truth in someone as unorthodox as Jesus.

What did they hear that we don't hear? Why did the earth quake under their feet when we don't feel a stirring of any sort? A part of the reason is that we have taken the shock value out of most of the parables. When Jesus tells the story about a truly good neighbor, the hero is a despised Samaritan, not a local rabbi (Luke 10:25-37). Suppose Jesus told us that story today and made the hero a Muslim? What would our reaction be? Now you feel the earthquake!

Suppose Jesus told us a story about "Guess Who's Coming to Dinner?" Well, he did (Luke 14:15-24). And when he gets through with the story, all the good, righteous people are NOT at the table and all the wrong people are seated at God's great Kingdom table.

---

1 Sue Monk Kidd, *When the Heart Waits* (San Francisco: HarperOne, 1990), 8.
2 Eugene Peterson, *Tell It Slant* (Grand Rapids: William. B. Eerdmans, 2008), 20.

Now you feel the earthquake! Suppose Jesus told a story about the end of time and the final separation of those who are "in" and those who are "out." Well, he did (Matthew 25:31-46). It's a parable parable that I title: "Surprise! Surprise! Surprise!" Those who are convinced they are sheep find themselves cast into outer darkness and those who sure look like goats to us find they are the recipients of eternal life. Now you feel the earthquake!

Even Jesus' disciples had to keep asking, "What did you mean by that parable?" They didn't know how to listen for larger truth because they kept their truth in a carefully guarded place. So do most of us. Compare the following two quotes:

> "One of the moral diseases we communicate to one another comes from huddling together in the pale light of an insufficient answer to a question we are afraid to ask."
> — Thomas Merton.[1]

> "I owe a lot here to two people. One is my former pupil and great friend Andrew Shanks, who kept on asking me awkward questions." — Rowan Williams.[2]

Listening to awkward questions and finding truth in unorthodox places does not mean that you throw overboard everything you believe. For me, it has meant that truth has become deeper and larger. My faith today is not less than it was when I began my ministry, it is much more. And, yes, it is more inclusive. It is more ecumenical. I have not been called upon to abandon any of my core beliefs in order to live in our present culture of differing voices. However, it is from some of those differing voices that I have learned a great deal.

1) **Exercise:** Have any significant insights in your faith journey come from an unorthodox source? Describe the insights and how they came.

---

[1] Quoted in Timothy Jones, *Awake My Soul* (New York: Doubleday, 1999), 25.
[2] Quoted in Rupert Shortt, *God's Advocates* (Grand Rapids: William B. Eerdmans, 2005), 16.

2) **Exercise:** Have you been in places where you were afraid to ask the real questions you wanted to ask? How did that make you feel?

3) **Exercise:** Discuss this quote:

> The Christianity I accept is found in the compassion of Mother Teresa, the intelligence of Reinhold Niehbuhr, the artistic rigor of Flannery O'Connor, the social activism of Martin Luther King, Jr., the evangelical fervor of Billy Graham, and the courage of Bonhoeffer.[1]

4) **Exercise:** How do you feel when you read these lines?:

> … I feel no need to deny other religious traditions to reaffirm my own….No one knows the limits of God's grace.[2]

THE OUTSIDER INTERVIEWS

Most church related people simply shake their heads in disbelief when they learn that the fastest growing segment of the religious population in America is called the "nones." This is the group that replies, "None," when asked about their religious affiliation. Most of them consider themselves to be spiritual with a belief in God and an active prayer life. They no longer see church membership as a necessary ingredient in their spiritual lives. And many of them are young adults.

The Outsider Interviews by Jim Henderson, Todd Hunter, and Craig Spinks is eye and ear opening in helping us to understand what Christianity looks like from an outsider's perspective. In the Forward to the book, David Kinnaman (President of the Barna Group) writes: "For all our communication abilities, we don't listen very well."[3] He's right. Most of us have no idea how those outside

---

[1] David S. Awbrey, *Finding Hope in the Age of Melancholy* (Boston: Little Brown, 1999), 20.
[2] Ibid, 220-221.
[3] Jim Henderson, Todd Hunter, and Craig Spinks, *The Outsider Interviews* (Grand Rapids: Baker Books, 2010), 12-13.

see and feel about the church. Wouldn't it help us in having real conversations if we did?

> More than one outsider told us they were shocked Christians were actually listening to them. Klarisa, an outsider in Kansas City, tore our hearts out when she said, "If Christians would listen and show some interest in me, I would be very open to their story." What if evangelism in our time is more about listening than speaking?[1]

One section in the book comes from a slogan used many years ago. It's not a bad slogan for our time: "Anchored to the Rock... Geared to the Times."[2]

QUESTIONS FOR REFLECTION AND DISCUSSION

1. What are some of the best questions you have heard recently?

2. How are some of the ways in which we might cultivate the discipline of noticing?

3. How do you interpret Frederick Schmidt's suggestion that "to listen well is to listen with the ears of others as well as our own"?

4. Do we usually feel the earthquake of Jesus' parables? Why not?

5. What could be the value of The Outsider's Interviews to your congregation?

---

1 Ibid, 22.
2 Ibid, 53.

Reflection Is Not an Option

THE BIBLICAL WITNESS

> *It is a snare for one to say rashly, "It is holy," and begin to reflect only after making a vow.* (Proverbs 20:25)

> *Just as it is written in the Law of Moses, all this calamity has come upon us. We did not entreat the favor of the Lord our God, turning from our iniquities and reflecting on his fidelity.* (Daniel 9:13)

> *Think over what I say, for the Lord will give you understanding in all things.* (2 Timothy 2:7)

> *But now more than ever the word about Jesus spread abroad; many crowds would gather to hear him and to be cured of their diseases. But he would withdraw to deserted places and pray.* (Luke 5:15-16)

CONTEMPORARY WISDOM

Reflection is essential for growth, development, and change. It is the unique power of the human person. Holding the cup of life means looking critically at what we are living.[1]

In the end, educators best serve students by helping them be more self-reflective. The only way any of us can improve…is if we develop a real ability to assess ourselves. If we can't accurately do that, how can we tell if we're getting better or worse?[2]

…[W]e are so overstressed and overburdened by our endless preoccupation with email and cell phones and iPods and multitasking, with no time left for critical reflection or the nurture of an intentional life of freedom and imagination.[3]

MULLING IT OVER

My father had a favorite response whenever we asked for something that we knew would call for a difficult decision on his part. He would say, "Let me mull that over." Without much formal education, but as an avid reader, he had learned the value of what he also termed cogitating or pondering. He never referred to what he did as reflecting but that is a good summary term for what he did.

However you tag it, both personally and as church we should be aware of the constant need to mull over, cogitate, ponder, reflect. Most of us could profit from a little Quaker silence in our meetings. Although we probably question the wisdom of the charge brought against one of Mozart's works in the movie Amadeus, we can use the idea to great advantage. "Too many notes" is an unfair criticism of that particular piece of music but the charge of "too many words" can be brought against many of our discussion sessions. There is

---

1 Henri Nouwen, *Can You Drink The Cup?* (Notre Dame: Ave Marie Press, 1996), 27.
2 Randy Pausch, *The Last Lecture,* 112.
3 Walter Brueggemann, *Disruptive Grace* (Minneapolis: Fortress Press, 2011), 88.

In Changing Times

too little time to process what is being said; opposing ideas come thick and fast with little time for sifting and weighing.

A simple, "Let's take five minutes for reflection," would correlate with what I once read about the British navy's three minutes of silence before making a decision about a current crisis. The soft drink slogan, "the pause that refreshes," could be experienced as we granted a respite from the cacophony of verbiage. Will some feel uncomfortable with five minutes of "nothing" going on? Truth be told, there could be a great deal going on; this time of reflection might well be the most crucial part of the meeting.

This could also be termed the time for "hushing."

> A psychotherapist of my acquaintance, Eric Maisel, whose practice is devoted to people in the arts who are struggling with the vicissitudes of that blood sport, has a technique he calls "hushing".... it's a quieting and an opening. Hushing is unfortunately easier said than done.
>
> Sitting quietly, hushing, for even a few minutes a day gives us a place in which to catch our breath, and a chance for our callings and intuitions to catch up with us.[4]

THE POWER OF SILENCE

While we hear much about the power of words, we hear little about the power of silence. The typical worship service in evangelical churches has little or no place for silence. "People don't know what to do with it" is the reason most often given for its avoidance. My response: "Then let's teach them what to do with it!" In a world that bombards our senses with constant high level noise, what could be more refreshing than to have a time and a place where we can find the off switch?

> No life can afford to be too busy to close the doors on chaos regularly; twenty minutes a day, two hours a week, a morning a month.[5]

---

4 Gregg Levoy, *Callings*, 25-26.
5 Joan Chittister, *Illuminated Life* (Maryknoll: Orbis Books, 2008), 61-62.

The reason most experience unease with silence at church is because they do not practice it in their daily lives. Good workshop question: After your daily Bible reading and prayer, how much time do you spend in silence and reflection? Collecting and reporting on the unsigned answers to this question would be quite revealing. (Recently, I read that only eleven percent of professing Christians practice daily Bible reading.) Good workshop discussion questions are: What value do you see in a regular time for reflection? What would be your suggestions for beginning such a practice?

I have often been asked about my normal Sunday morning routine and when I tell people I get up around 5:00 a.m. they are shocked. "Do you need that much time to get your sermon ready?" is usually what they ask. My response is: "No, I need that much time to get myself ready." Some worship folders will contain the phrase "Preparation for Worship." I contend this is what needs to be done before people arrive for the service. What difference do you think it would make if each of those attending spent only a few minutes of time at home in reflective preparation for worship?

HOW COULD JESUS PRAY SO MUCH AND FOR SO LONG?

The citation from Luke is only one of many Gospel references to Jesus' prayer life. It is a consistent priority in the ministry of the one about whom it was said, "We've never before seen anything like what he does; we've never before heard anything like what he says." To simply say, "Well, after all, we do believe he was the Son of God," is not a sufficient answer. After Jesus' baptism, the temptation account in Luke concludes with: *When the devil had finished every test, he departed from him until an opportune time* (4:13). The issue in the temptation narrative relates to the kind of Messiah Jesus will be, the kind of ministry and mission he will have. Luke lets us know this was a continuing temptation from the tempter as well as from the crowds and Jesus' own disciples. They appear to have had the same kind of Messianic job description Jesus initially and continually rejected.

The disciples must have had some sense of the power of Jesus' prayer life. Their request, "Teach us to pray," resulted in what we call The Lord's Prayer or The Disciples' Prayer. Its brevity is astonishing when you stop to consider the volumes that have been written in an attempt to interpret it. Surely Jesus did more than repeat this brief prayer during his all night prayer vigils. Surely he did more than pray some of the psalms. Surely he did more than fill his prayer time with words. Surely he spent a great deal of time in listening and reflecting.

If he was tempted in all points such as we are (Hebrews 4:15), then many times he must have asked, "Am I doing exactly the things I ought to be doing? Is my emphasis in the right place? Am I being true in every way to my Father's mission? Should I try to make peace with the Pharisees and religious leaders? Are there places I can compromise? Am I being too provocative by healing on the Sabbath?" Whether these were the exact questions or not, every time Jesus reappeared following his withdrawal for prayer, he was clearly focused on who he was and what he was about.

Workshop question: What do you think Jesus did during his extended times of withdrawal from the crowds and from his disciples?

THE PLACE OF KNOWING

> Safe in the magic of my woods I lay
> And watched the dying light
> Faint in the pale high solitudes
> And washed by rain and veiled by night.
> Silver and blue and green were showing
> And the dark wood grew darker still
> Wind was hushed and peace was growing
> And quietness crept up the hill.
> I knew this was the hour of knowing.[1]

After citing this poem, Douglas Weaver writes: "There are some things we shall never know until we are quiet, until we listen

---

1 Rupert Brooke, cited in Douglas Weaver, *From Our Christian Heritage*, 61.

to our hearts."[1] "Where is your place of knowing?" is always a relevant question. It is one of the questions we need to keep asking ourselves. Sharon Daloz Parks charges that we live in a state of "systemic distraction" that is encouraged by the very structures of contemporary postmodern life.[2]

Workshop assignment: Sometime during this week, take one hour and go to a shopping mall or a busy intersection. Observe the people (and if at an intersection, the cars) and make notes of the ways people are distracted from being present where they are and with what they are doing. (On a recent errand, I noted that almost fifty percent of drivers were talking on cell phones. One almost ran me off the road and seemed to be unaware that he had done so.)

The awareness of systemic distraction is a wakeup call for regular times for reflection.

> Interiority, the making of interior space for the cultivation of the God-life, is the essence of contemplation.... Going into the self, finding the motives that drive us, the feelings that block us, the desires that divert us, and the poisons that infect our souls brings us to the clarity that is God.... We make space for reflection. We remind ourselves of what life is really all about. We tend to the substance of our souls.[3]

Where is the place of knowing about the motives that drive us, the feelings that block us, the desires that divert us, and the poisons that infect our souls? To acknowledge that I need to know these things is the first step. These are the things that drive my life and my ministry. Frederica Mathewes-Green has written: "Repentance is not blubbering and self-loathing. Repentance is insight."[4] I agree. Only insight can bring about a change of mind and a change of direction (the biblical meaning of the word *repent*).

---

1 Ibid.
2 Quoted in Nancy Malone, *Walking a Literary Labyrinth* (New York: Riverhead Books, 2003), 73.
3 Joan Chittister, *Illuminated Life,* 61.
4 Quoted in Fleming Rutledge, *Not Ashamed of the Gospel* (Grand Rapids: William B. Eerdmans, 2007), 336.

During my times of reflection, I often ask myself: "Why did I react to that so quickly? What caused me to feel the way I did when I heard that remark? Why do I really want to have that position? What is it I really want? What do I really believe to be my major task in this ministry? Why am I often so short with the persons I love the most?" These are but a sampling of the many things that come up for reflection (most as uninvited guests!). If I take seriously the feedback I get from my family, my friends, my work, and my world then I will have plenty of material to mull over. If I get it even half way right, it becomes a key place for knowing.

ANYONE FOR BIBLICAL AND THEOLOGICAL REFLECTION?

The Psalter opens with the blessings that come to those who meditate day and night on the law of the Lord (Psalm 1:2). These persons are compared to trees planted by streams of water; they never wither because they are watered and rooted in biblical and theological assurances. Daniel 9:13 warns of the dangers of failing to reflect on God's fidelity (faithfulness in the past and commitment in the presence). This is a call for biblical and theological reflection.

Workshop exercise: What is your understanding of the meaning of these terms? Redemption; Incarnation; Atonement; Election; Salvation; Conversion; Baptism; Second Coming; Revelation; Eschatology; Lord's Supper; Trinity; Covenant.

The above list should be adapted to suit your particular church. One purpose of such an exercise is to reveal the lack of biblical and theological understanding that is pervasive in our churches. Contrary to what often has been suggested, I believe we need to reintroduce a biblical and theological vocabulary in our preaching and teaching. In the days of regular Sunday night services, nothing killed attendance like announcing a doctrinal series. All too often such series were dry as dust. This is not what I am suggesting.

"Make it interesting and make it relevant" is always my watchword when preparing a sermon. Being true to the text means that when people depart from the service they will have a little better understanding of a particular portion of Scripture and a better grasp of some pertinent theology. When I was graduated from the seminary one of the charges I received was: "In your pastorate with all else you will be called upon to do, don't neglect being the theologian in residence." That's what I have always tried to be. If the people in my congregation did not get some biblical and theological teaching from me, where were they going to get it? And if they did get it from other sources, where were they going to discuss it? Where were they going to find a place to do a little group reflection?

An emphasis on the gospel as story has led some to believe that sermons ought to be inspirational stories. I hope people will feel inspired when my sermon is over but I also trust that the inspiration will have content and focus that come from a biblical text. There ought to be content that helps build a solid faith with a biblical and theological foundation. Does this take time and hard work? You bet it does!

Workshop question: Thinking over the past few months of sermons, what are the particular biblical and theological insights that have meant the most to you in your faith and daily living?

For Pastors: Keep a notebook and for each week's sermon make a notation of the biblical and theological truths you have attempted to communicate to your people. How varied are they? How comprehensive are they?

WE CAN CHOOSE, WE CAN DECIDE

Sometimes I go about my activities with senses dulled, like the man who ran into the Louvre Museum in Paris, breathless, blurting out, "Quick, where's the *Mona Lisa*? I'm double-parked outside."[1]

To confess that this described me in many of my pastorates is to tell but half; if I am not careful, I can quickly slip back into the breathless mode. Being a type A person has not made it easy to practice what I preach about listening, being present, taking time, carefully observing, and pausing to reflect. The man in the quote may have been able to "see" the *Mona Lisa*; he would not have "experienced" the Mona Lisa.

---

1 Timothy Jones, *Awake My Soul* (New York: Doubleday, 1999), 69.

Most of the things we do or refrain from doing are the result of our decisions and our choices. If we are honest, some of the choices and decisions are those that help us avoid asking hard questions to ourselves.

> A wag has said that Freud's central insight into the human psyche can be summed up in the notion that the truth about ourselves is a secret we keep from ourselves.[1]

This is the secret that no one can give you. You have to make the discovery for yourself. If you are like me, you have found that this is an ongoing discovery and is never total or complete. One of the great sources for learning the truth about ourselves is reflection.

One writer has this take on it: "It is that sense of effortless inner conversation that I am interested in helping you discover."[2] If you are having trouble with the concept of reflection, think of it as a time of inner conversation. A suggestion that might seem strange is to talk to yourself aloud (make certain no one else is around!). Why not? Verbalizing what you are feeling and thinking can be very clarifying. Why should this seem so strange? I loved Alan Alda's book *Things I Overheard While Talking To Myself*. The title alone is worth the price of the book because to reflect means that I begin to overhear things while talking to myself.

> (We) are bombarded with messages that everyone is sending and to which few are listening. Often referred to as the "information age," our era is unlikely ever to merit the label the "age of wisdom." Wisdom comes from listening, from observing. Wisdom presupposes a process of discernment, of weighing and sifting.[3]

If we are to have time for discernment, weighing, sifting and gaining some real wisdom, then reflection is not an option.

---

1 Gerald Janzen, *At the Scent of Water* (Grand Rapids: Eerdmans Publishing, 2009), 89.
2 Frederick Schmidt, *What God Wants For Your Life*, 133.
3 Ibid, 140.

QUESTIONS FOR REFLECTION AND DISCUSSION

1. How much time do you set aside regularly for reflection? What has been its value?

2. How would you describe the power of silence?

3. What is your "hour of knowing"?

4. What are some "Mona Lisa" experiences you have had? Why?!

5. What things have you overheard while talking to yourself?

10

Major on Conversation, Candor, and Compassion

THE BIBLICAL WITNESS

> *They said to each other, "Were not our hearts burning within us while he was talking to us on the road, while he was opening the scriptures to us?"* (Luke 24:32)

> *And after Paul and Barnabas had no small dissension and debate with them, Paul and Barnabas and some of the others were appointed to go up to Jerusalem to discuss this question with the apostles and the elders.* (Acts 15:2)

> *Therefore, let us celebrate the festival, not with the old yeast, the yeast of malice and evil, but with the unleavened bread of sincerity and truth.* (1 Corinthians 5:8)

> *Have I become your enemy by telling you the truth?* (Galatians 4:16)

> *…[S]peaking the truth in love, we must grow up in every way into him who is the head, into Christ….* (Ephesians 4:15)

Stand therefore, and fasten the felt of truth around your waist, and put on the breastplate of righteousness. (Ephesians 6:14)

When he saw the crowds, he had compassion for them, because they were harassed and helpless, like sheep without a shepherd. (Matthew 9:36)

As God's chosen ones, holy and beloved, clothe yourselves with compassion, kindness, humility, meekness, and patience. (Colossians 3:12)

CONTEMPORARY WISDOM

Tag-line communication, called "bite-speak" by some, is destroying the last remnants of political discourse; spin doctors and media consultants are our new shamans.[1]

In healthy congregations, information flows freely.[2]

As Richard Hofstadter reminds us, America was founded by intellectuals, a rare occurrence in the history of modern nations. "The Founding Fathers," he writes, "were sages, scientists, men of broad cultivation, many of them apt in classical learning, who used their wide reading in history, politics, and law to solve the exigent problems of their time."[3]

In a cartoon, an older man is sitting across the desk from an agency person who asks him, "Do you prefer to be called

---

1 Sven Birkets, *The Gutenberg Elegies*, 123.
2 Peter L. Steinke, *Healthy Congregations* (Herndon, VA: Alban Institute, 1996), 9.
3 Neil Postman, *Amusing Ourselves To Death* (New York: Penguin Books, 2005), 41.

'Geriatric,' 'Elderly' or 'Senior'?" With a heavy frown, the man responds, "I prefer to be called Mr. Stevens."[1]

> Though we have not, of course, reached agreement, we are satisfied that we have eliminated misunderstandings, that is, that neither of us has misrepresented the other. We offer the result to the reader as the celebration of shared friendship, faith, and scholarship.[2]

WORDS DEFINED

By using the word "candor" in between "conversation" and "compassion," I mean the primary definition given by *Webster's New World College Dictionary*: "openness, the quality of being fair and unprejudiced, impartiality." I am not using it in the secondary sense: "sharp honesty and frankness in expressing oneself." Those who pride themselves on being "brutally honest" often come down heavily on the side of brutality and sharpness. This is one of the best ways I know to stop conversation. By conversation I mean dialogue (discussed below) and by compassion I mean viewing every person as a human being created in the image of God.

Here is an activity question: What have you experienced as the primary barriers to dialogue (conversation, talking together) in your church? Do you have any suggestions as to how these barriers might be removed (or least lowered)?

Over a decade ago Joseph Phelps wrote *More Light; Less Heat*. In this book he gives ten guidelines for dialogue:

1. Risk: moving beyond our fears of the unknown and trusting that God will be there to undergird us.

2. Respect: granting that the image of God is present in all people and being willing to grant them this honored place, even when we cannot see it in them with our own eyes.

---

[1] William J. Carl, ed., *Graying Gracefully* (Louisville: Westminster John Knox, 1997), 7.
[2] Marcus J. Borg and N. T. Wright, *The Meaning of Jesus* (New York: HarperCollins, 1999), xi.

3. Fairness: releasing the temptation to get the upper hand by any means available, and trusting the process enough to grant an adversary a level playing field for the give and take of ideas.

4. Humility: owning one's limitations in every area of life.

5. Teamwork: looking for the Holy Spirit in the most unexpected places.

6. Openness: being willing to learn.

7. Listening: recognition that God is at work in other places.

8. First-person speech: recognizing that God is at work in you.

9. Depth: believing that God's truth has levels of complexity and meaning that humanity will never fully comprehend.

10. Patience: understanding that we are part of a long lineage of people who have sought to discern the will of God in community, and finding the grace to humbly place our part.[3]

TURN DOWN THE HEAT

In a conflict situation, one of my primary objectives is to lower the temperature. The term "inflammatory remarks" has a biblical basis: *How great a forest is set ablaze by a small fire! And the tongue is a fire* (James 3:5b-6a). The old saw, "Sticks and stones may break my bones but words will never hurt me," is simply not true. Words can roast you alive; they can destroy your church. James contends that self-discipline begins with controlling our tongues (3:2). The best way I know to begin lowering the temperature in any conflict is to eliminate the blowtorch words, the words that put others on the defensive, the words that demean or put down, the words that make the situation win/lose, the words that make us the authorities, the words that are framed as answers instead of questions.

As if it were not already bad enough, in the election year of 2012 the examples of how not to dialogue are everywhere. What

---
3 Joseph Phelps, *More Light; Less Heat,* 168.

most disturbs me is how many people see nothing wrong with any of this because it is purported to be "communication." The bottom line is usually that they agree with the person speaking and do not have plans to listen to any other point of view. Many see themselves equipped for their personal "defend and destroy" mission. Alas, this cuts across all party and religious lines.

In attempting to turn down the heat in relationships, one writer cites two greeting cards he found. One reads: "Let's be friends again – too many foolish mistakes cost us our friendship. Now that time has passed, I know we can put aside our differences." Another reads: "I'm not angry – I'm just out of sorts. Please send more sorts."[1] A major task for the pastor is to keep handy a good supply of "sorts," both for himself and members of the congregation.

Question: what are the "sorts" that immediately come to your mind?

ON READING THE OUTRAGEOUS

The word outrageous in the above heading should be in quotes; I'm referring to something that seems outrageous to us. Something with which we disagree so strongly that we are at a loss to see how anyone could believe it. Something that is in complete opposition to what we believe. Something that is at the opposite end of the spectrum. There are two major reasons for reading the "outrageous."

The first is that you will never understand a position or point of view unless you hear it from someone who holds it and is able clearly to articulate it. The problem with most discussions is that an opposing point of view is usually presented in a totally unsympathetic manner coupled with the use of the worst examples. It is given only to reveal how absurd, ridiculous, or unorthodox it is. A fair hearing is nowhere in sight.

The second reason for reading the outrageous is that in order to engage in productive dialogue I must be fully aware of my disagreements with another position at its best. A caricature is all

---

1   Charles Klein, *How To Forgive When You Can't Forget* (Bellmore, NY: Liebling Press), 52.

too often presented as "the other point of view" and provides no grounds for exploration and discovery. If we ever hope that someone on the other side of things might see merit in our side we must be willing to at least see the possibility of learning something from that which we disagree! (I hesitate to put such statements in print because they need to be unpacked in a workshop.)

In the Bibliography of Quoted Sources you will find a wide variety of books. Most of the references are written by "solid" Christian writers; some are by authors who hold less than "orthodox" positions on some matters; two are by agnostics; one is by an atheist. One of the agnostics confesses that he lost his belief in a good and just God after the suicide of his older son and the leukemia death of his younger son all in a little over a year's time. The other agnostic notes his earlier career as a *Youth for Christ* speaker (to huge crowds) and a personal friend of Billy Graham. He confesses that he can no longer believe what he once preached. He is now an atheist because he cannot imagine there being a God when there is so much evil in the world.

Much of my reading has to do with "doing church" in this postmodern world. As a church consultant and intentional interim minister I want to know what is going on in the church world even if I can never envision it going on in my world. I have read several books on the emerging church and have just finished reading a book by two who are opposed to the entire movement and make a mixed case for their position.

Somewhere I read that "light is light regardless of who is holding the candle." This sounds like heresy to many. How can a heretic have anything to say that I would want to hear? How could anything of value come from the pen of an atheist? The answer to both of those questions is: often a great deal! Note: this does not mean that everything remains subject to alteration or deletion. It does not mean that I lack conviction or confidence in what I believe.

IS ONE "TRUTH" JUST AS GOOD AS ANOTHER?

I am fully aware of the attacks on "conversation," "discussion," and "dialogue" as the abandonment of one's own beliefs and convictions. This attack correlates "tolerance" with the idea that one truth is just as valid as another; tolerance means I concede "truth" is simply in the eye of the beholder. This is not what I mean by discussion, dialogue, conversation. The Christian faith must have content; doctrine is a necessary part of any belief system. Everything rests on something.

For two decades Harvey Cox taught a course at Harvard titled "Jesus and the Moral Life." His book, *When Jesus Came to Harvard: Making Moral Choices Today*, is an account of his dialogical method of teaching the course. He writes:

> Among the hundreds of students who took Jesus and the Moral Life during the two decades I taught it, many came from serious, often quite pious, Christian families. They often questioned some of my interpretations of the Bible, but I encouraged them to stand up for their convictions.[1]

He summarizes the two most important values of discussion in two sentences:

> The discussion had done two things. They had taught them to present their beliefs in a more coherent way, and had pushed them into reexamining even their firmest convictions, to think it possible "that they too might be mistaken."[2]

The words in quotes refer to Oliver Cromwell's well-known letter of 1650 to the Assembly of the Church of Scotland in which he said, "I beseech you, in the bowels of Christ, think it possible you may be mistaken." Cox then quotes Judge Learned Hand who said he wished these words could be inscribed "over the portals of every church, every school, every court house, and, may I say, every single legislative body in the United States."[3]

Apologetics is usually thought of as "the branch of theology having to do with the defense of the proofs of Christianity" (*Web-

---

1 Harvey Cox, *When Jesus Came to Harvard* (Boston: Houghton Mifflin, 2004), 259.
2 Ibid, 297.
3 Ibid, *296.*

ster's New World College Dictionary). In a broader sense, it has to do with presenting the case for the Christian faith. Its worst examples are often seen in those who are certain they are God's Defenders, the Guardians of the Faith, the Protectors of Orthodoxy and those who don't agree are the enemy (or worse, instruments of the demonic). Too many of us have been exposed to those who simply wish to shout us down, pound the truth into us, show us how wrong we are and how right they are, and threaten us with eternal consequences if we ignore their teachings.

KEEPING ONE EYE ON THE RELATIONSHIP

> "I am not against technology so much as I am for community. When the choice is between the health of the community and technological innovation, I choose the health of the community." — Wendell Berry.[1]

In presenting what I believe to be some truths of the Christian faith, I am always concerned about the health of the community in which I am speaking; I am always concerned about the quality of relationships. This is not a matter of watering down my beliefs or a "peace at any price" attitude. Even before reading it, I had adopted the position advocated by Peter Leithart: "Instead of an agenda, I propose a stance, a stance of faith, joy, and celebration in the midst of postmodern mist."[2]

In my three previous books, I have tried to outline my theological positions, basic approach to biblical interpretation, and the concrete specifics of the gospel on which I base my faith. I do not have a nebulous "anything goes" philosophy about what I have been preaching, teaching, and learning for over fifty years. If I have any regrets (and I do!) it is that frequently I let my convictions and enthusiasm override my compassion for those to whom I was speaking. I failed to keep an eye on the relationship which always

---

[1] Joel Shuman and Roger Owens, eds., *Wendell Berry and Religion* (Lexington: University of Kentucky, U of K Press, 2009), 23.
[2] Peter Leithart, *Solomon Among the Postmoderns*, (Grand Rapids: Brazo Press, 2008), 14.

In Changing Times

has almost everything to do with the receptivity of your message. When we are told that Jesus looked at the crowds with compassion, it logically follows that they welcomed and listened to his teachings.

Keeping one eye on the relationship is illustrated in the admonition: "When looking at the artwork of a child, we are told, do not ask, 'What is it?' Instead, say, 'Tell me about it.'"[1]

Dan Merchant in his highly controversial (and frequently banned!) book, *Lord, Save Us From Your Followers*, has identified four primary ways that have become the accepted ways we communicate our ideas, both through the media and in person:

> *Myopia* – our communication conveys our point of view exclusively. While our facts may be accurate, we lack context and, ultimately, understanding by ignoring any information that doesn't put forward our agenda.
>
> *Hyperbole* – our communication again conveys our point of view, but we exaggerate the facts and distort the available information to create an intellectually dishonest and, possibly, more persuasive case for our agenda.
>
> *Hysteria* – our communication conveys our point of view in an emotional and aggressive manner based primarily on our feelings, what we want to be true, and our blind desire to be right and see our agenda come to fruition.
>
> *Truth* – our communication conveys as balanced a review of the facts as possible, including the weaknesses of our position and the strengths of the other's. The goal of this communication is the illumination of reality and, in this case, our agenda considers the well-being of all people, not just those who agree with us. It's tough to fit this on a bumper sticker.[2]

---

[1] W. Paul Jones, *Trumpet At Noon* (Louisville: Westminster/John Knox, 1992), 125.
[2] Dan Merchant, *Lord, Save Us From Your Followers* (Nashville: Thomas Nelson, 2008), 15.

LET'S TALK ABOUT IT

> ...[T]he community of faith in which and from which we live finds its self-awareness only through our speaking with each other. Our community of faith is a community of communication. It is a community of dialogue, or perhaps we should say, of multilogue.[1]

If there is any "secret" to what I do, it is working to create a safe, non-threatening, structured environment in which people feel free to talk with one another. It takes time for this to happen. Usually there has to be a rebuilding of trust, the establishment of guidelines that prevent sabotage, and the experience of sessions in which talking with each other becomes a pleasant and profitable experience. Conflict ridden churches rarely look back on times when they talked together. When they listened together. When they shared their stories and insights – without interruption or comment. I really believe that genuine conversation in church can be called "truth seeking understanding."

The biggest shock during an intentional interim is usually when the members of a congregation discover that, in large measure, they really don't know one another. Knowing another person makes all the difference in how you listen (how you hear) what they have to say. Many fear an intentional interim is all about "touchy-feely" stuff and that they will be forced to talk when they don't want to. They fear it might be an "Oprah Live." It is not. I never call on anyone for a response and the right to remain silent is always a given.

"Let's talk about it" is the call for clarification and understanding. It does not always mean that opinions will change or that an immediate resolution is reached. Even if these don't happen, people will leave the meeting with much less frustration and a greatly diminished level of anxiety. Often the "conclusion" reached is: "We may not agree on this but it appears we can find ways to work with one another."

---

1 James Adams, *An Examined Faith* (Boston: Beacon Press, 1991), 366.

A PRACTICAL AND HELPFUL RESOURCE FOR TALKING ABOUT IT

John Lepper has recently written an excellent (and, as far as I know, a one of its kind) workbook titled *Building Bridges During the Interim: A Workbook for Congregational Leaders*. (The workbook is available from the publisher, Nurturing Faith, Inc., Macon, GA, www.nurturingfaith.net, Barnes and Noble, and Amazon.)

The author outlines its intended usage:

> The target audience is congregational leaders. They may or may not serve on the search committee. They may or may not serve as deacons or elders…. These congregations run the gamut from small country churches to larger city churches. Some have no ministry staff other than the pastor, and others are multi-staff congregations. Lay leaders who might find this book useful include: Church Council, Elders, The Session (Presbyterian), Consistory, Leadership Team – by whatever name, Deacon Body, Personnel Committee.

Under his Purpose statement, Lepper writes:

> The purpose of this book is to help lay, congregational leaders understand the dynamics of congregations during the interim…. This workbook seeks to help you, a lay leader, answer two questions regarding the interim: (1) What can I expect? (2) What can I do?

The chapter titles provide the best overview of the content:

1. Providing Leadership in Times of Anxiety
2. Understanding the Congregation-Family Connection
3. Saying Goodbye to the Past
4. Appreciating Our Past
5. Determining Our Identity
6. Filling the Gaps of Leadership

7. Relating to Our Denomination and Other Groups
8. Seeking New Leadership
9. Saying Hello to the Future
10. Dealing With Unexpected Situations

QUESTIONS FOR REFLECTION AND DISCUSSION

1. How do you think it can be helpful to group "conversation, candor, and compassion" together?
2. What is your take on Joseph Phelp's ten guidelines for dialogue?
3. What are the "sorts" you need in a congregation to keep the heat turned down?
4. What are some of the most helpful "outrageous" articles and books that you have read? In what ways were they helpful?
5. Which of Dan Merchant's four primary ways of communicating ideas do you find the most used in the church? Do changes need to be made?

Conclusion
Insights from the Book of Proverbs

In an intentional interim I have the advantage of preaching on Sundays. Sermons in the context of worship help provide a biblical basis for what I am attempting to do in the workshops and discussions that follow. Congregations are usually comfortable with something they perceive to be biblical; most are unhappy with anything seen as the latest fad in church psychology.

Some of the ideas in this book may appear to be on the radical edge so I am concluding with insights from a portion of what is termed the wisdom literature of the Old Testament. Largely ignored in preaching and Bible studies, there is much practical advice for contemporary churches struggling to find their place in a world gone "post" in just about everything. My selections are not meant to be exhaustive but hopefully will send you on your own search into Proverbs for wisdom that is timeless.

These proverbs make excellent discussion starters; they are listed under the chapter to which they best apply. (All are from the New Living Translation Bible.)

CHAPTER 1: TRUTH IS ONLY THE BEGINNING OF THE JOURNEY

Teaching the Teachable

Proverbs 9:8-9 *Do not rebuke mockers or they will hate you; rebuke the wise and they will love you. Instruct the wise and they will be wiser still; teach the righteous and they will add to their learning.*

Not everyone is teachable; not everyone is ready to be a part of the solution instead of remaining a part of the problem. Not everyone responds to what is done in an intentional interim. Some will choose not to participate in discussions and workshops. Rather than attempting to recruit the unrecruitable, I focus on the most motivated members of the congregations, on those who are ready to move forward.

Hasty Decisions Often Carry a High Price Tag

Proverbs 19:2 *Zeal without knowledge is not good; a person who moves too quickly may go the wrong way.*

"Are we ready to make a decision?" is a question the overly zealous may not want to hear. Determining the pace of things is not always easy but it is always a crucial ingredient in any successful endeavor.

CHAPTER 2: IT'S THE BIG PICTURE THAT PROVIDES PERSPECTIVE

The Prescription for Playfulness

Proverbs 17:22 *A cheerful heart is good medicine, but a broken spirit saps a person's strengths.*

"I am so glad we are able to once again laugh together" is a frequent comment in the course of an interim. Phrased in different ways, people tell me that the atmosphere is different and things don't seem nearly as serious as they once did. On a few occasions, I have seen cheerful hearts filled with laughter function as nothing less than a miracle cure.

CHAPTER 3: CONTROL IS IN SHORT SUPPLY

Being a Non-Anxious Presence

Proverbs 12:16 *A fool is quick-tempered, but a wise person stays calm when insulted.*

Proverbs 15:1 *A gentle answer turns away wrath, but harsh words stir up anger.*

The challenge to be a thermostat instead of a thermometer is the challenge for every member of a congregation. The temptation to react instead of to respond never goes away. Thinking about the atmosphere we want to create rather than the point we want to make is a good place to begin.

There Is No Way to Eliminate Risk

Proverbs 22:13 *The lazy person is full of excuses, saying, "If I go outside, I might meet a lion in the street and be killed."*

Playing it safe is really not playing it at all. Life is a risky business to begin with and anything we undertake involves some risk. Degrees of risk vary but "risk zero" has no possibilities.

The Future Belongs to God

Proverbs 27:1 *Don't brag about tomorrow, since you don't know what the day will bring.*

I have written an entire book subtitled *Mastering the Art of Letting Go*. The thesis of that book is that we are in charge of input and God is in charge of outcome. We do what we believe we are called to do (both as individuals and as churches) and then we let it go. Volumes have been written on the theme of our not knowing what the future holds but of knowing the One who holds the future. Proverbs 27:1 is the call to trust that God is faithful and that even if tomorrow brings the unexpected or worse, God's faithfulness remains the bedrock of our security.

CHAPTER 4: BELIEFS AND ATTITUDES SHAPE OUR WORLD

The Heart of the Matter

Proverbs 4:23 *Above all else, guard your heart, for it affects everything you do.*

Psalm 139:23-24 *is a sobering parallel passage: Search me, O God, and know my heart; test me and know my thoughts. Point out anything in me that offends you, and lead me along the path of everlasting life. (NLT)*

The Hebrew term for *heart* is rendered *mind* in some translations. *Heart* in Hebrew means all that is within me – my heart, my mind – all that I am. Keeping in touch with our hearts is no easy matter. Guarding our hearts means that we will attempt to be aware of what is shaping the way we see things, the way we feel about things, the way we react to things. Some helpful questions are: "Why did I react so strongly to what was said?" "Why does this issue raise such anxiety in me?" "Why can't I let go of something that happened so long ago?" "Why do 'certain' people give me such concern?" "Why did I have such a knee-jerk reaction to that comment?"

In working with conflicted churches, I place a great deal of emphasis on making discoveries through reflection and conversation with trusted persons. The first question to ask is not, "What is going on in our church?" but "What is going on in me?" Only after we have begun that process do we then seek to let others tell us how and why they see and feel about things as they do. Some call this telling our own stories and listening to the stories of others. This is a good place to begin in attempting to understand ourselves and others.

CHAPTER 5: FORGET ABOUT PERFECTION

A Messy Job Anyway You Look At It

Proverbs 14:4 *An empty stable stays clean, but no income comes from an empty stable.*

Never let it be said that the Bible shies away from the earthiness of life. I hesitate to state the obvious: a stable full of horses produces a stable full of stuff to shovel out. It comes with the territory. Too many believe that if we are all Christians then church is the last place where there is little, if any, conflict. A common assumption is that the messiness of life should never intrude into the Kingdom plans of God's saints. To believe this is a possibility one needs, first of all, to ignore the New Testament letters to churches. Are love, family, church, community, and basic relationships worth all the stuff we have to put up with? Absolutely! So we keep shoveling!

Learning to Live With Imperfections

Proverbs 17:9 *Disregarding another person's faults preserves love; telling about them separates close friends.*

The New Testament has no model for the perfect church; the model is rather one that calls for ongoing forgiveness and reconciliation. It is the struggle for integrity and the necessity of continuing to "grow in Christ" that was the challenge then and now. There is no way to eliminate faulty people from our congregations; those are the only kind of people there are.

CHAPTER 6: THE DANGERS IN LISTENING FOR THE APPLAUSE.

Don't Toot Your Own Horn

Proverbs 27:2 *Don't praise yourself; let others do it!*

"Don't toot your own horn" is one of the many clichés my father learned from his father and passed on to me. Whenever I have used this in a workshop someone inevitably protests, "But what if no one toots your horn?" My response is always the same, "Then you remain tootless!" After the laughter subsides, we have some very interesting discussions.

Constructive Evaluation

Proverbs 29:1 – *Whoever stubbornly refuses to accept criticism will suddenly be broken beyond repair.*

Jesus is the only one I know who always got it "right." The rest of us are in need of regular evaluation and course correction. In our personal lives and in the life of the congregation, many wait until things are *broken beyond repair* before seeking help. Providing structure for regular and appropriate evaluation (criticism) is one of the most difficult and necessary ingredients for healthy relationships.

CHAPTER 7: LIFE IS FULL OF ENDINGS

Fixing the Vision

Proverbs 4:25 *Look straight ahead, and fix your eyes on what lies before you.*

"How much time will we spend thinking about and discussing our past?" is a frequently asked question as I begin an interim ministry. My basic answer is: "Only as much time as it takes to make certain nothing in the past prevents the church from moving ahead." Comments such as: "I know how he really feels," "That has never worked for us before," "She wouldn't say that if she had experienced what I went through," "They are asking me to forget what is still fresh in my mind," "It still hurts too much to say it is all forgiven," are telling statements that much work needs to be done with things that are past but still very much alive.

A shared, hopeful vision for the future is the best context I know for creative and productive discussion. The interim task is to help the church get ready for a new minister and a new future. Paul's admonition to a church in Philippians 3:13-14 is the New Testament version of Proverbs 4:25:

> ...[T]his one thing I do: forgetting what lies behind and straining forward to what lies ahead, I press on toward the goal for the prize of the heavenly call of God in Christ Jesus.

Timing, Timing, Timing

Proverbs 25:11 *Timey advice is as lovely as golden apples in a silver basket.*

The right word at the right time cautions against right words at just any time. It's another take on "when the pupil is ready the teacher will come." Knowing when to say it, to whom to say it, how to say it, and in what situation to say it – this is the art of golden apples in a silver basket.

CHAPTER 8: WE NEED EYES THAT SEE AND EARS THAT HEAR

On Being Willing to Listen

Proverbs 18:13 *What a shame, what folly, to give advice before listening to the facts!*

Proverbs 18:17 *Any story sounds true until someone sets the record straight.*

Paul Harvey's famous phrase "the rest of the story" is often the most neglected part of many church stories. I cannot count the number of people who have said to me, "I had no idea that some of the members of our church felt that way."

CHAPTER 9: REFLECTION IS NOT AN OPTION

Finding What We Are Looking For

Proverbs 11:27 *If you search for good, you will find favor; but if you search for evil, it will find you!*

This is the way of majoring on strengths in a congregation, of doing asset-based planning, of emphasizing gifts and possibilities, of refusing to focus on problems and "fixes."

CHAPTER 10: MAJOR ON CONVERSATION, CANDOR, AND COMPASSION

Speaking the Truth in Love

Proverbs 28:23 *In the end, people appreciate frankness more than flattery.*

Empty flattery is never a part of my interims; specific affirmations are. People know when you are just "laying it on thick." (To be noted: the purpose of most flattery is for the benefit of the flatterer.) I have never worked with a congregation that wanted me to be dishonest with them. They wanted true and forthright assessments of where they were and how they were doing. This proverb is tied closely to the one found in Proverbs 29:1: *Whoever stubbornly refuses to accept criticism will suddenly be broken beyond repair.*

Bibliography of Quoted Sources

Adams, James. *An Examined Faith.* Boston: Beacon Press, 1991.

Adams, Scott. *The Dilbert Principle.* New York: HarperCollins, 1996.

Adler, Bill. *Dear Pastor.* Nashville: Thomas Nelson, 1980.

Alda, Alan. *Things I Overheard While Talking to Myself.* New York: Random House, 2008.

Awbrey, David S. *Finding Hope in the Age of Melancholy.* Boston: Little Brown, 1999.

Barnette, Henlee. *A Pilgrimage of Faith.* Macon: Mercer University Press, 2004.

Birkets, Sven. *The Gutenberg Elegies.* New York: Facwett Combine, 1994.

Blackburn, Richard. *Leadership and Anxiety in the Church.* Lombard, IL: Lombard Peace Center, 2007.

Blanchard, Ken. *The Heart of a Leader.* Tulsa: Honor Books, 1999.

Bondi, Roberta. *In Ordinary Time.* Nashville: Thomas Nelson, 2002.

Borg, Marcus and Wright, N. T. *The Meaning of Jesus.* New York: HarperCollins, 1999.

Bossidy, Larry and Charan, Ram. *Execution.* New York: Crown Business, 2002.

Boteach, Shmuley. *Renewal.* New York: Basic Books, 2010.

Bradberry, Travis and Greaves, Jean. *The Emotional Intelligence Quick Book.* New York: Simon & Schuster, 2005.

Brooks, David. *The Social Animal.* New York: Random House, 2011.

Brueggemann, Walter. *Disruptive Grace.* Minneapolis: Fortress Press, 2011.

Buechner, Frederick. *Secrets in the Dark.* San Francisco: HarperOne, 2006.

Burke, Spencer. *A Heretic's Guide to Eternity.* San Francisco: Jossey-Bass, 2006.

Capps, Donald. *A Time to Laugh: The Religion of Humor.* New York: Continuum Publishing, 2005.

Carl, William J. Editor. *Graying Gracefully.* Louisville: Westminster John Knox, 1997.

Carpenter, Candice. *Chapters.* New York: McGraw-Hill, 2002.

Chittister, Joan. *Illuminated Life.* Maryknoll: Orbis Books, 2008.

Coffin, William Sloane. *Credo.* Louisville: Westminster John Knox, 2004.

Couglin, Paul. *No More Christian Nice Guy.* Minneapolis: Bethany House, 2005.

Cowan, John. *The Common Table.* New York: HarperBusiness, 1993.

Cox, Harvey. *When Jesus Came to Harvard.* Boston: Houghton Mifflin, 2004.

Crysdale, Cynthia. *Embracing Travail.* New York: Continuum, 2001.

Epstein, Fred. *If I Get to Five.* New York: Henry Holt, 2003.

Felber, Terry. *Am I Making Myself Clear?* Nashville: Thomas Nelson, 2002.

Fields, Rick. *Chop Wood Carry Water.* Los Angeles: Jeremy P. Tarcher, 1984.

Finley, James. *Merton's Palace of Nowhere.* Notre Dame: Ave Maria Press, 1978.

Fox, Michael J. *Always Looking Up.* New York: Hyperion, 2009.

Friedman, Edwin. *A Failure of Nerve.* New York: Seabury Books, 2007.

Fuller, Robert C. *Religious Revolutionaries.* New York: Palgrave Macmillan, 2004.

Garland, David and Diana. *Flawed Families of the Bible.* Grand Rapids: Brazos Press, 2007.

Goldberg, Philip. *Roadsigns on the Spiritual Path.* Boulder: Sentient Publications, 2006.

Gordon, Josh. *Presentations That Change Minds.* New York: McGraw-Hill, 2006.

Greeley, Andrew. *Myths of Religion.* New York: Warner Books, 1989.

Hall, Douglas John. *Thinking the Faith.* Minneapolis: Augsburg, 1991.

Henderson, Jim; Hunter, Todd; Spinks, Craig. *The Outsider Interviews.* Grand Rapids: Baker Books, 2010.

Hollis, James. *Why Good People Do Bad Things.* New York: Gotham Books, 2007.

Janney, Rebecca Price. *Who Goes There?* Chicago: Moody Publishers, 2009.

Janzen, J. Gerald. *At the Scent of Water.* Grand Rapids, Eerdmans Publishing, 2009.

Jones, Timothy. *Awake My Soul.* New York: Doubleday, 1999.

Jones, W. Paul. *Trumpet at Noon.* Louisville: Westminster/John Knox, 1992.

Kabat-Zinn, Jon. *Wherever You Go There You Are.* New York: Hyperion, 1994.

Kelly, Matthew. *Perfectly Yourself.* New York: Ballantine Books, 2006.

Kendall, R.T. and Rosen, David. *The Christian and the Pharisee.* New York: Faith Words, 2006.

Kidd, Sue Monk. *When the Heart Waits.* San Francisco: HarperOne, 1990.

Kinnaman, David. *You Lost Me.* Grand Rapids: Baker Books, 2011.

Klein, Allen. *The Courage to Laugh.* New York: Jeremy P. Tarcher/Putnam, 1998.

Klein, Charles. *How To Forgive When You Can't Forget.* Bellmore, NY: Liebling Press.

Kuhn, Clifford. *The Fun Factor.* Louisville: Minerva Books, 2002.

Kushner, Harold. *The Lord Is My Shepherd.* New York: Alfred A. Knopf, 2003.

Leithart, Peter. *Solomon Among the Postmoderns.* Grand Rapids: Brazo Press, 2008

Lesser, Elizabeth. *The New American Spirituality.* New York: Random House, 1999.

Levoy, Gregg. *Callings.* New York: Three Rivers Press, 1997.

Lord, Walter. *A Night to Remember.* New York: St. Martin's Griffin, 2005.

Malone, Nancy. *Walking a Literary Labyrinth.* New York: Riverhead Books, 2003.

Merchant, Dan. *Lord, Save Us From Your Followers.* Nashville: Thomas Nelson, 2008.

Monks of New Skete. *In the Spirit of Happiness.* Boston: Little Brown, 1999.

Norris, Kathleen. *Acedia & Me.* New York: Riverhead Books, 2008.

Nouwen, Henri. *Can You Drink the Cup?* Notre Dame: Ave Maria Press, 1996.

O'Brien, Mary. *Successful Aging.* Concord, CA: Biomed General, 2005.

Opie, Iona and Peter. *I Saw Esau.* Cambridge: Candlewick Press, 1992.

Pausch, Randy. *The Last Lecture.* New York: Hyperion, 2008.

Peterson, Eugene. *Tell It Slant.* Grand Rapids: William B. Eerdmans, 2008.

Phelps, Joseph. *More Light; Less Heat.* San Francisco: Jossey-Bass, 1999.

Postman, Neil. *Amusing Ourselves to Death.* New York: Penguin Books, 2005.

Prather, Hugh. *The Little Book of Letting Go.* New York: MJF Books, 2000.

Raschke, Carl. *The Next Reformation.* Grand Rapids: Baker Academic, 2004.

Rohr, Richard. *The Naked Now.* New York: Crossroad Publishing, 2009.

Rutledge, Fleming. *Not Ashamed of the Gospel.* Grand Rapids: William B. Eerdmans, 2007.

Schmidt, Frederick. *What God Wants For Your Life.* New York: HarperCollins, 2005.

Shortt, Rupert. *God's Advocates.* Grand Rapids: William B. Eerdmans, 2005.

Shuman, Joel and Owens, Roger, Editors. *Wendell Berry and Religion.* Lexington: University of Kentucky Press, 2009.

Snyder, Howard. *Decoding the Church.* Grand Rapids: Baker Books, 2002.

Sparks, Susan. *Laugh Your Way to Grace.* Woodstock: Skylight Paths Publishing, 2010.

Steinke, Peter L. *Healthy Congregations.* Herndon, VA: Alban Institute, 1996.

Swears, Thomas R. *Preaching to Head and Heart.* Nashville: Abingdon Press, 2000.

Sweet, Leonard. *Postmodern Pilgrims.* Nashville: Broadman & Holman, 2000.

Tickle, Phyllis. *The Great Emergence.* Grand Rapids: Baker Books, 2008.

Tippett, Krista. *Speaking of Faith.* New York: Penguin Books, 2008.

Tuleja, Tad. *Quirky Quotations.* New York: Galahad Books, 1992.

Vallet, Ronald E. *Stewards of the Gospel.* Grand Rapids: William B. Eerdmans, 2011.

Wallis, Jim. *Call to Conversion.* San Francisco: HarperOne, 2005.

Weaver, Douglas, Editor. *From Our Christian Heritage*. Macon: Smyth & Helwys, 1997.

Welshons, John and Carlson, Richard. *When Prayers Aren't Answered*. Novato, CA: New World Library, 2007.

About the Author and the Offer of Free Workshops

The author, Ron Higdon, is a certified church consultant with over fifty years of pastoral and interim ministry experience. His published works include: *From Fear to Faith: The Spiritual Journey from Anxiety to Trust; But If Not: Mastering the Art of Letting Go; In the Meantime: Learning to Live in Difficult Times* (all published by Parson's Porch Books), and *Surviving a Son's Suicide*.

Except for expenses, workshops on this book are offered free of charge. The only requirement is that participants purchase the book. You can contact the author by email: rbooks5000@aol.com, by telephone: 502-228-5431, or by writing him at 6224 Deep Cove Court, Prospect, KY 40059.

Also by Ronald Higdon

Other parents will give thanks for Ron Higdon's brave book and bless his name in the middle of many a dark and wooly night.

Dr. John Killinger

More from Energion Publications

Personal Study
Holy Smoke! Unholy Fire	Bob McKibben	$14.99
The Jesus Paradigm	David Alan Black	$17.99
When People Speak for God	Henry Neufeld	$17.99
The Sacred Journey	Chris Surber	$11.99

Christian Living
It's All Greek to Me	David Alan Black	$3.99
Grief: Finding the Candle of Light	Jody Neufeld	$8.99
My Life Story	Becky Lynn Black	$14.99
Crossing the Street	Robert LaRochelle	$16.99
Life as Pilgrimage	David Moffett-Moore	14.99

Bible Study
Learning and Living Scripture	Lentz/Neufeld	$12.99
From Inspiration to Understanding	Edward W. H. Vick	$24.99
Philippians: A Participatory Study Guide	Bruce Epperly	$9.99
Ephesians: A Participatory Study Guide	Robert D. Cornwall	$9.99
Ecclesiastes: A Participatory Study Guide	Russell Meek	$9.99

Theology
Creation in Scripture	Herold Weiss	$12.99
Creation: the Christian Doctrine	Edward W. H. Vick	$12.99
The Politics of Witness	Allan R. Bevere	$9.99
Ultimate Allegiance	Robert D. Cornwall	$9.99
History and Christian Faith	Edward W. H. Vick	$9.99
The Journey to the Undiscovered Country	William Powell Tuck	$9.99
Process Theology	Bruce G. Epperly	$4.99

Ministry
Clergy Table Talk	Kent Ira Groff	$9.99
Out of This World	Darren McClellan	$24.99

Generous Quantity Discounts Available
Dealer Inquiries Welcome
Energion Publications — P.O. Box 841
Gonzalez, FL 32560
Website: http://energionpubs.com
Phone: (850) 525-3916

www.ingramcontent.com/pod-product-compliance
Lightning Source LLC
LaVergne TN
LVHW041625070426
835507LV00008B/454